Animal Assisted Therapy

CTAC METHOD

Techniques and Exercises for
Dog Assisted Interventions

Eva Domènec ■ Francesc Ristol

SMILES
CTAC
·publishing·

Animal Assisted Therapy
CTAC Method
Techniques and Exercises for
Dog Assisted Interventions

1st edition, December 2012

Copyright © 2012

Authors:
Eva Domènec
Francesc Ristol

Publisher:
SMILES CTAC Inc.
2655 Le Jeune Road
Coral Gables, FL 33134

www.smilesctac.com
Email: info@smilesctac.com

Illustrator: Marta Perdigó
Translator: Douglas Mine

ISBN 978-0-9886331-0-0
Library of Congress Control Number: 2013905131

Index

Foreword

With great pleasure, I am happy to introduce this book on techniques and exercises for dog assisted interventions by Eva Domènec and Francesc Ristol of CTAC. The authors respect the definitions of animal-assisted interventions given by the International Society for Animal-Assisted Therapy on www.aat-isaat.org and follow the guidelines and resolutions of the International Association of Human-Animal Interaction Organizations, IAHAIO, on www.iahaio.org . But they draw upon their vast practical experience of working with patients/clients at Barcelona's Sant Joan de Déu Hospital and provide therapists as well as volunteers with many ideas on how to successfully work with well-behaved, healthy dogs.

Many people have a desire to do that, their motivation is high, but they don't know how to get started or what to do with the dogs once there! Several years ago, the authors of this book were in the same boat! Now, they have put their accumulated knowledge on paper, and in a very easy-to-use format, to help others get started. This exercise book will also give the therapeutic staff of other hospitals, clinics and further social institutions suggestions on how to work together with the dog handlers to improve the abilities and wellbeing of their charges.

I commend the authors of this work for "a job well done" and wish all readers success in developing their own programs to help other persons benefit from such activities.

Switzerland, November 2012

PD Dr. sc. Dennis C. Turner
Delegate of the IAHAIO
Board on European Issues
Secretary of the International Society for
Animal-Assisted Therapy, ISAAT

Who could have known...

...that today I'd be here with my therapy dogs Cuca and Bamba in the gardens of San Joan de Déu Hospital waiting to begin a session of cognitive stimulation with animal assisted therapy.

I've reached this point thanks to the personal, professional and entrepreneurial growth I've experienced alongside Francesc Ristol, and to all those who have taken part in the assisted therapy with dogs.

Francesc and I first set out on this journey working with a group of wonderful boys and girls named Pecus, Javi, Isa, Xavi and Campru, all of whom have Down syndrome. With our Spanish Water Dogs Nadal, Bruixa and Mel, among others, we did animal assisted activities while immersed in particularly beautiful surroundings: our "Can Llosses Center" in the nature reserve of Collserola outside Barcelona.

With this group, and bolstered by our theoretical and therapeutic know-how, it was a sure thing that Pecus and his friends were in for something good. We had the kids, the dogs, the therapists and the desire... Only one thing was missing: discovering just the right activities that could motivate these young people to work day after day with the dogs, to interact with nature and relate to each other in order to achieve the individual and group goals we'd established at the outset.

Finding the right activities seemed, back then, a task as simple as going to a specialized bookstore and selecting a book of exercises and activities that included the participation of animals. Believe me when I tell you that this continues to be one of my missions: finding that book to help us enrich the field of animal-assisted therapy.

But since we didn't find that book, we thought we should share our accumulated knowledge by giving professional training courses for future experts and technicians in animal-assisted therapy, and by publishing what you now hold in your hands: CTAC's first book dedicated specifically to exercises in animal-assisted therapy.

This first book is a collection of basic exercises for employing social skills, getting comfortable with the dog, interacting as a group, basic cognitive stimulation and psycho-motor activity.

Because two is better than one, a third always follows the second and two plus two equals four, this volume will be followed by three others with more-specialized exercises in the following areas: sensory stimulation, cognitive stimulation and, finally, a compendium of exercises grouped according to the different programs that we here at CTAC have carried out over the years.

There's no doubt that we agree on one thing: therapy is much more effective when there's motivation for doing it. As Levinson said: "the best way to communicate is by playing." So then, Let's play! Let's work! Let's work by playing!

I invite you to share your dog's love and playfulness with those whose faces and hearts will light up upon seeing him

Eva Domènec
Coordinator of the
AAI Programs of CTAC

Introduction

of the Animal Assisted Interventions Unit of

Barcelona's Sant Joan de Déu Hospital

Barcelona's Sant Joan de Déu Hospital is a private non-profit medical center that works in concert with the public healthcare system and is associated with the University of Barcelona (Spain).

It is a state-of-the-profession facility in pediatrics and Ob-Gyn, and enjoys a high international ranking with regard to admissions, capacity and discharges (22,000 annually).

Our mission and institutional values are reflected in a long-term strategic plan called Paidhos, an acronym alluding to the Greek word Paidós (child) while defining and synthesizing our most basic precepts: Professionalism, Accessibility, Innovation, Instruction, Hospitality, Organization, Solidarity and Sustainability.

Our concept of care is based on the individual patient. We put it into practice by way of our program Hospital Amic (Hospital Friend), which was created to enshrine the fundamental principles of the European charter of the Rights of Hospitalized Children and the principle of Hospitality of the San Juan de Dios religious order.

With that in mind, San Joan de Deú Hospital strives to embody Innovation and the use of therapeutic instruments that help us provide the best care possible for our patients, adapting to their ways of communicating and interpreting reality.

We include in this context our Animal Assisted Interventions, which we've been using for more than two years with very satisfying results. Judging from the empirical evidence provided by our own center and others using similar programs, we have clearly demonstrated the effectiveness of these interventions with our patients.

The process begins with health professionals observing the needs of a patient and the obstacles to be overcome in his treatment or care. It is they who decide whether Animal Assisted Intervention can be a useful tool. Then an expert (a healthcare professional) and a technician determine which sort of intervention is called for in light of the therapeutic objectives. At the conclusion of each intervention, they make a joint evaluation of how it was implemented and what results were achieved. In so doing we contribute to the continuous improvement of the interventions and the constant raising of standards in the various programs.

That is how a program originally designed for a particular type of patient – children and adolescents with mental health problems – has grown and broadened its scope to the point of becoming a unit unto itself that provides services to all the medical departments and specializations that can benefit from them. The goal is to provide help and stimulus to children and young people struggling to overcome their problems and to adapt to the circumstances and challenges posed by their condition. In order to do that, we healthcare professionals join forces with the wonderful creatures that are the dogs, along with the technicians who work with them, to improve strategies in all general areas and optimize personalized care in each particular case, with evident positive results

Francisco Javier Lozano Olea
Coordinator of the
Animal Assisted Interventions Unit of
Barcelona's San Joan de Déu Hospital

Animal Assisted Interventions

REASONINGS BEHIND THE DECISION TO REPLACE THE TERMINOLOGY
ANIMAL ASSISTED THERAPY WITH THAT OF ANIMAL ASSISTED INTERVENTIONS

If we look back through history, we see that a close relationship between man and various animal species has existed for thousands of years. Furthermore, the employment of domesticated animals in therapeutic programs has been around for quite a while. That said, the extensive, organized and documented use of such techniques is relatively recent. Consequently, if we look at different publications in our field, we find varying terminology describing our profession: canine therapy, co-therapist, animal assisted therapy, etc.

There are many definitions of Animal Assisted Therapy. A.M. Beck says AAT is "therapy that implies the use of animals as therapeutic agents." A.H. Katcher describes it as "the utilization of the therapeutic capacity of contact with animals" and Granger and Kogan go by the Delta Society's definition, which refers to "an intervention that pursues a curative objective and which uses the person-animal bond as an integral part of the treatment process."

As the Delta Society says, Animal Assisted Activities (AAA) – as distinguished from Animal Assisted Therapy (AAT) – have as their objective the improvement of the individual's quality of life through the use of the person-animal bond, but are not administered by a therapist and are not documented or evaluated differently from other interaction with animals.

In publications, manuals, articles, lectures and courses on Animal Assisted Therapy, we currently find the following phrases and acronyms referring to the interaction between people and animals:

> AAA   Animal Assisted Activities
> AAT   Animal Assisted Therapy
> AAE   Animal Assisted Education

While drafting the Interventions Protocol for dogs to be used in ITAKA, the psychiatric unit of Barcelona's Sant Joan de Déu Hospital, the following reflections and questions arose:

On one hand, we felt that too many terms are included under the rubric of Animal Assisted Therapy (AAT), including those from AAI, which had already comprise so-called Animal Assisted Therapies (plural), though in this case from the point of view of the therapeutic interaction with the patient, or "user."

On the other hand, we asked ourselves if we used in the heading the word therapy in its clinical sense, would AAA, AAE or the Resident Programs be out of place under that umbrella? In order to provide an answer to this question, and with the intention of a more specific use of terminology, we proposed substituting the word therapy in the heading Animal Assisted Therapy (AAT) with the word interventions, making it Animal Assisted Interventions (AAI), considering that this nomenclature more accurately describes and better comprises the various kinds of interaction between people and animals.

We must keep in mind that this change affects all the abbreviations we will be using from now on. With the use of interventions instead of therapy, the abbreviations or acronyms for the people involved also change. The person previously referred to as the Receiver of Therapy (RT) becomes the Receiver of the Intervention (RI), or the "user" benefitting from the AAI sessions.

The Therapy Professional (TP) becomes the Intervention Professional (IP), the health or education professional whose academic formation and experience has provided him or her with the knowledge for administering interventions.

What was previously called the Assisted Therapy Technician (ATT) becomes the Assisted Intervention Technician (AIT). He or she is the professional responsible for the handling and the physical and emotional wellbeing of the animal before, during and after the AAI sessions. This person's main goal is fostering positive and productive interaction between the RI and the animal.

A new term is that of the Intevention Unit (IU), a pairing made up of an AIT and an individual animal specifically trained and selected for use in an AAI session.

Summing up: **Animal Assisted Interventions (AAI)** are classified according to the professionals involved in the conception, development, execution and evaluation of the session. With that in mind, we divide the AAI in five categories:

AAA – Animal Assisted Activities:
The Intervention Unit (IU) directs the session for one or more users (RIs) with the aim of achieving overall objectives previously established by the team responsible for the group.
In other words, **AAA= IU+RI(s)**.

AAT – Animal Assisted Therapies:
The Intervention Unit (IU) works throughout the session alongside a health professional (IP) so that the dog functions as a facilitator, a motivator or a support mechanism for the Receiver of the Intervention (RI) who then makes progress in an enjoyable and accelerated way toward achieving of the previously established therapeutic objectives.

Included in this rubric are professionals in Psychiatry, Neurology, Psychology, Nursing, Physical Therapy, Occupational Therapy, etc., all those who, according to their degrees and licenses for clinical practice, perform a function designed to achieve agreed-upon objectives. So, **AAT= IU+IP+RI.**

AAE – Animal Assisted Education:

The Intervention Unit (IU) works throughout the session with an education therapist (IP) so that the dog functions as a facilitator, motivator or support mechanism for the RI, who makes progress in an enjoyable and accelerated way toward achievement of the previously established educational objectives. **AAE= IU+IP+RI**

AAEv – Animal Assisted Evaluation:

The Intervention Unit (IU) works with the RI's inter-disciplinary team. The team, depending on its focus, takes advantage of the interaction between the RI and the animal to evaluate a diagnosis or treatment program.
Thusly, **AAEv= IU+inter-disciplinary team+RI.**

ARP- Animal Resident Programs (PAR):

The animal resides permanently in a center and takes part in the daily life of the users. This animal is specifically trained as a therapy animal and can participate in other AAIs in the same center.

CHART SHOWING THE NEW CLASSIFICATION

Presented by Francesc Ristol at the 1st International Congress on Animal Assisted Therapy in Rehabilitation organized by the Corporación de Ayuda a la Familia de Carabineros de Chile (Santiago, Chile, September 7, 2011).

		Participants in the intervention			
				IU	
		IR	IP		
	Intervention name			AIT	Dog
ANIMAL ASSISTED INTERVENTIONS (AAI)	AAA	X		X	X
	AAT	X	X	X	X
	AAE	X	X	X	X
	AAEv	X	X	X	X
	ARP	X			X

The key to success in AAI: The RI's bond with the dog

Erik Erikson, an American psychologist known for his work in the psychology of human development, made an important contribution to understanding the relationship between human beings and their pets. He said that it is deeply influenced by the individual's early formative stage, by his or her previous experiences and, in infancy, by the attitudes expressed toward dogs or other animals by the person's parents and grandparents.

As professionals in the field of Animal Assisted Interventions, we must work on behalf of the positive consolidation of the bond between animal and human being and – in the specific case of the CTAC – between the dog and the Receiver of the Intervention, or the RI.

When we do an AAI, the first objective is that the RI feels relaxed with the dog's presence in the room. The degree of proximity and interaction will be established by each individual participant; we must be able to interpret his or her body language in order to proceed accordingly. Moving too fast or in an improvised way do not create a solid foundation for working toward our goals.

In order to create a stable bond and positive dynamic between the RI and the animal we must proceed step by step with their interaction. That way we can increase the degree of autonomy the RI has in handling the dog and, consequently, his own self-esteem. If the RI feels loved, competent and able, how easy it will be for him to work towards therapeutic goals alongside his canine companion.

Here below are listed various patterns that can appear during an intervention, and the kinds of behavior that must be re-directed if they show up during interaction. The list is not intended to provide a chronological sequence of behavior we will necessarily see, because each RI is a different individual. But it can help us to better understand just where we are, and where we want to go.

Grooming area

The RI:
- does not make eye contact with the dog when they are more than 3 feet apart.
- makes eye contact with the dog when they are more than 3 feet apart.
- remains alert while grooming the dog at a safe distance.
- grooms the dog in a relaxed way while continually reducing the distance between them.
- relaxed, begins grooming the dog on his own.
- grooms the dog using both hands.
- grooms the dog and is able to follow simple instructions.
- grooms the dog and is able to follow complex instructions.
- begins and completes the grooming on his own.
- is able to guide a companion in the dog's grooming.

Behavior that must be re-directed:
- The RI uses the grooming tools on himself.
- The RI uses the grooming tools incorrectly.
- The RI brushes the coat too vigorously or in the wrong direction.

Giving Treats

The RI:
- does not want to touch the treats.
- tosses the treat to the dog from a distance of more than 3 feet without eye contact.
- tosses the treat to the dog from a distance of more than 3 feet with eye contact.
- places the treat on the Intervention Professional's palm more than 3 feet away from the dog and observes its delivery.
- places the treat on the IP's palm less than 3 feet away from the dog and observes its delivery.
- places the treat on a tray and presents it to the dog.
- places the treat on the palm of his own hand and presents it to the dog with the aid of the IP.
- places the treat on the palm of his hand and presents it to the dog without help.
- holds the treat between two fingers (tweezer-style) and presents it to the dog with help.
- holds the treat between two fingers and presents it to the dog without help.

Behavior that must be re-directed:
- The RI wants to try eating a treat.
- The RI performs a repeated or stylized action with the treat before presenting it and giving it to the dog.

Contact

The RI:
- is anxious about the dog with the animal in the "stay" position more than 3 feet away.
- is relaxed with the dog in the "stay" position more than 3 feet away.
- is anxious about the dog with the animal in the "stay" position less than a meter away.
- is relaxed with the dog in the "stay" position less than 3 feet away.
- is anxious about the dog in movement less than 3 feet away.
- is relaxed with the dog in movement less than 3 feet away.
- exhibits anxiety while superficially petting the dog with his fingertips.
- in a relaxed way, pets the dog with both hands and initiates movement.
- remains relaxed while seated beside the dog and touches, caresses or other wise maintains contact with him.
- lays down and relaxes on top of the dog.

Behavior that must be re-directed:
- The RI tends to harshly manipulate the dog with hands or feet.
- The RI wants to treat the dog like a pony (tries to "ride" him).
- The RI grabs the dog inappropriately.

The leash and the walk

The RI:
- is reluctant to take hold of the dog's leash.
- takes the leash in a light grasp and holds it briefly.
- throws the leash on the ground each time the IP gives it to him.
- continues to hold the leash with the IP's help.
- holds onto the leash by himself for ever-increasing periods of time.
- holds the leash with both hands.
- the RI's grip and control of the leash is such that he handles the situation even if the dog tugs on it.

- lets the dog lead and he follows.
- walks alongside the dog.
- sets the pace.
- transits courses and circuits with the dog.

Behavior that must be re-directed:
- The RI stereotyped handling of the leash (snapping, twirling).
- The RI brusque use of the leash.

Tossing and giving things to the dog

The RI:

– refuses to pick up or hold the object.
– takes hold of the object and gives it to the dog with the help of the IP but without eye contact.
– takes hold of the object to be given to the dog with the help of the IP but only if the object is dry.
– takes hold of the object to be given to the dog with the help of the IP even if it is wet.
– picks up the object after the dog has dropped it on the floor.
– placing his hand below the dog's lower jaw, accepts the object directly from the animal.
– takes the object directly from the dog's mouth.
– gives a verbal command or gesture for the dog to give him the object.

– refuses to toss the object to the dog but maintains attentive eye contact with him.
– gives the object directly to the dog.
– tosses the object at a distance of less than 3 feet.
– tosses the object at a distance greater than 3 feet.
– gives a verbal command or gesture for the dog to fetch the object.

Behavior that must be re-directed:

– The RI exhibits anxiety at the dog's movements.
– The RI will not pay attention to whatever the dog is doing.
– The RI exhibits impatience.

How to use this book

Over the course of these years CTAC has developed and put into practice myriad exercises in the field of Animal Assisted Interventions.

All of them have been documented, evaluated and employed by the various professionals with whom we've had the pleasure of sharing our work.

I can guarantee that each of these exercises has contributed to achieving, by way of play, previously established objectives and, above all, has brought a smile to the faces of many individuals who our dogs have had the pleasure of working with.

This book is intended as a guide for Animal Assisted Intervention professionals. In it, experts and technicians will find abundant ideas for creating new activities that enrich their work and help attain therapeutic and educational goals.

Each exercise has the following structure:

1– The activity and possible variations
2– Materials and commands employed in the exercise
3– A schematic drawing
4– Areas of endeavor and possible objectives

I wish that with these exercices you enjoy every minute of all the AAI sessions.

Welcome to CTAC METHOD, the treatment and educational model that changes the way clidren and adults are helped worldwide

Francesc Ristol
Director of CTAC Group

sensorial stimulation exercises

sensorial

stimulation

exercises

SELF-PORTRAIT

The game's objective is for the RI to draw his silhouette and the silhouette of the dog.

Sitting in front of the mirror, the individual closely observes the animal.

At first, from this position, the therapist can:

– Point out similarities and differences between the two.
– Ask the RI to touch a certain part of his body or the body of the dog.
– Ask him to touch on the mirror a certain part of his body or the body of the dog.
– Ask him to brush the dog, but while looking in the mirror rather than at the animal.
– Exercise the concepts of right and left with the use of handkerchiefs.

Next, we give the individual finger paint so that he can draw:

– The dog's silhouette on the mirror.
– A part of the dog's body in a certain color.
– His own silhouette.
– Finally, both the RI and the dog will leave their handprint and paw print on the mirror.

Variations:

– Place the dog and the RI face-to-face. The RI is asked to imitate the dog's posture and movements as if he were a mirror, copying each motion.

– Place the dog in front of the person, who most move the same side of his body that the dog does (e.g., right/right).

– The dog exhibits cards illustrating his various emotions. The person must represent that emotion, making a face or acting out.

COMMANDS FOR THE DOG	MATERIALS
• Up	• Mirror
• Bye-bye Right/Left	• Colored finger paints
• Sit	• Handkerchiefs
• Paw Right/Left	• Brush
• Stand	• Cards showing dog emotions
• Get it	
• Back/Come	
• Shame Right/Left	
• Twist Right/Left	

	Physical coordination	Objectives
Psychomotor Area	Sensory stimulation	• Exercise visual-space perception
	Space-time perception	• Exercise concept of right-left
	Corporal awareness	• Exercise balance
Cognitive Area	Atention and concentration	• Acquire or exercise notion of axis of symmetry
	Recognition of categories	• Imitate movements: body control
	Memory	• Pay attention to movements of others
	Language and communication	• Acquire or exercise ability to imitate
Social-emotional Area	Presentation	• Stimulate the imagination
	Activity	• Take pleasure in movement
	Leave-taking and relaxation	• Express feelings: sadness, happiness, anger
	Board games	• Experience the pleasure of controlling an object

The object of this game is to give a flower to the therapy dog.

Using construction paper or a thin sheet of foam rubber, we cut out the different parts of a flower: petals, the center, leaves and stem. We use Velcro or tape to attach the parts.

Every time the RI answers a question or carries out an instruction correctly, he will get a part of the flower that he can attach to the stem.

The dog waits patiently with the stem resting on his back until the RI completes the flower.

To earn a part of the flower, the RI can:

- Read a story and correctly answer questions about it.
- Ask or answer questions about feelings, preferences or things he likes.
- Recall a sequence of commands and have the dog obey them.
- Use face-making or mimicry to represent a person or thing so that other participants can guess who or what it is.
- Carry out a specific action: hug, caress, whisper...
- Overcome an obstacle on a course.

Once the flower is complete, the RI will take a walk to show off the dog and his flower. Lastly, we can disassemble the flower while doing things that promote relaxation.

COMMANDS FOR THE DOG	MATERIALS
• Sit • Stay	• Foam rubber rose attachable to the dog collar • Materials to be used in other activities

		Objectives
Psychomotor Area	Physical coordination	
	Sensory stimulation	• Exercise fine motor skills
	Space-time perception	• Recognize parts of a whole
	Corporal awareness	• Develop symbolic thinking
Cognitive Area	Atention and concentration	• Stimulate the imagination
	Recognition of categories	• Promote socialization
	Memory	
	Language and communication	
Social-emotional Area	Presentation	
	Activity	
	Leave-taking and relaxation	
	Board games	

TOUCH...CLICK...TREAT

The object of the game is for the RI to interact dynamically with the dog while following instructions given by the IP.

The IP first explains that the dog understands both spoken commands and commands given by hand signals. With the hands, the animal can be guided to any desired point. Every time the dog touches the palm of our hand with his snout, we will make a click with a clicker and give him a treat.

This exercise can be done in couples. One of the participants will make the hand signals and give the treat, while the other will make the clicks whenever the dog touches the partner's hand with his snout.

At the beginning, the RI's movements will be simple ones:

– Extend an arm to one side with an open hand but with fingers together.
– Alternate that movement from one arm to the other.
– Rest the palm of the hand against the thigh.
– Place the hand between the legs.

The partner clicks the clicker at the appropriate time, then the dog is given a treat.

Variations:

– Each movement will be repeated a pre-established number of times. Then, we can ask the RI to perform a simple choreography.

COMMANDS FOR THE DOG	MATERIALS
• Target: touch with his snout.	• Treats
	• Clicker

SENSORIAL STIMULATION

	Physical coordination	Objectives
Psychomotor Area	Sensory stimulation	• Exercise overall coordination
	Space-time perception	• Exercise hearing
	Corporal awareness	• Exercise concept of right-left
	Atention and concentration	• Develop sense of anatomy
Cognitive Area	Recognition of categories	• Exercise the sense of rhythm
	Memory	• Perceive signals by touch
		• Pay attention to movement of others
	Language and communication	• Acquire or exercise the capacity to concentrate
Social-emotional Area	Presentation	• Develop social interaction
	Activity	• Develop sense of teamwork
	Leave-taking and relaxation	
	Board games	

The objective of the game is for the RI to arrive at the finish line after interacting with the dog and employing the concepts of left and right.

We draw a starting line and a finish line and come up with an activity to be completed between them: put the hoops on a stake, assemble a puzzle, tell a story with images or writing, brush the dog...

To reach the finish line, the RI advances every time he extends his hand and the dog touches it with his snout (target).

We attach some adhesive labels to the RI's hands; a red one on the left and a green one on the right. Another option is for the RI to paint his hands red and green or, if working with a group, that the kids paint each others' hands.

The IP says either "red" or "green" and the RI extends that color hand for the dog to touch with his snout. At a certain point, the concept of "right" (green hand) and "left" (red hand) is introduced and those words become commands.

Each time the RI extends the correct hand the dog will touch it, allowing him to advance toward the finish line.

COMMANDS FOR THE DOG	MATERIALS
• Target right and left	• Red and green adhesive labels
	• Finger paint
	• Puzzles
	• Images
	• Brush

		Objectives
Psychomotor Area	Physical coordination	• Acquire or exercise the sense of direction; visual trajectory, right-left
	Sensory stimulation	
	Space-time perception	• Acquire or exercise the sense of space and direction
	Corporal awareness	• Exercise balance
Cognitive Area	Atention and concentration	• Exercise the notion of right-left
	Recognition of categories	
	Memory	
	Language and communication	
Social-emotional Area	Presentation	
	Activity	
	Leave-taking and relaxation	
	Board games	

The objective of this game is that the RI identifies and associates sensory perceptions.

He is presented with a series of three boxes, each one of which contains something that will produce a tactile, olfactory or taste sensation that will then be referred to the world of the dog.

In the olfactory series, the first box holds a sponge soaked in baby's cologne; the second, an onion, and the third, a cloth imbued with the scent of a dog.

The RI then smells the dog, after which he smells each of the boxes to determine which contains the element smelling most like the dog. Another option is putting the dog treats in one of the boxes.

In the tactile series, the boxes contain: one, sawdust; two, water; three, dog hair. To start, the RI pets the dog, after which he puts his hand into each of the boxes and is then asked which contains the material most similar to the dog's coat. Another possibility is placing a pumice stone in one of the boxes, as a material similar to the paw pads of the dog.

In the taste series, the RI must identify, by taste, the dog's favorite food or another food indicated by the IP. The IP gives the RI pieces of food, and when the RI correctly identifies the food the IP named at the outset, he is allowed to give a piece of food to the dog.

Variations:

– The RI identifies each box, with or without illustrative cards. When he is right, he can tell the dog to do a trick and give him a treat.

– Once the RI knows and memorizes the sequence of the three elements in a series, he commands the dog to find the box containing a specific material. The RI must say whether the dog's choice was correct or not before the box's contents are revealed.

COMMANDS FOR THE DOG	MATERIALS
• Down	• Three boxes or containers
• Stay	• Various foods
• Treat	• Scented items
• Search	• Items of diverse texture
	• Illustrative cards

32

	Physical coordination	Objectives
Psychomotor Area	Sensory stimulation	• Exercise fine motor skills
	Space-time perception	• Exercise hand-eye coordination
	Corporal awareness	• Exercise the sense of touch
Cognitive Area	Atention and concentration	• Exercise the sense of taste
	Recognition of categories	• Exercise the sense of smell
	Memory	• Develop language: expression and comprehension
	Language and communication	• Acquire or exercise sense of direc tion: visual trajectory, right-left
Social-emotional Area	Presentation	• Acquire or exercise mental concentration
	Activity	• Develop or evaluate visual memory
	Leave-taking and relaxation	• Recognize parts of a whole
	Board games	• Learn to listen and respond

Upon completing an activity, the RI will get a piece of molding clay (Playdough or similar). He will use this to make a souvenir of his friend, the therapy dog, and will put finishing touches on the piece.

At first, we can help the RI to perceive the tactile sensation produced by the clay, comparing it with the sensation of feeling the dog's coat.

The RI must work out the best way for the dog to effect a "handshake": depending on the size of the animal, he will either raise the paw to the clay or place the piece of clay on the floor or ground beneath the dog's paw. We will then apply gentle but firm pressure on the leg in order to leave a good paw print in the clay.

The RI then uses different materials and tools to decorate the print and write his own name and that of the dog. Once the clay is dry, he can paint or varnish the piece as a finishing touch.

COMMANDS FOR THE DOG	MATERIALS
• Stay • Sit • Paw	• Molding clay • Treats • Colored bunting • Colored pebbles • Paint or varnish • Tools for working clay

SENSORIAL STIMULATION

	Physical coordination	Objectives
Psychomotor Area	Sensory stimulation	• Cooperation: Stimulating teamwork
	Space-time perception	• Sensory stimulation
	Corporal awareness	• Enhance tactile recognition
	Atention and concentration	• Experience the pleasure of getting messy
Cognitive Area	Recognition of categories	• Experience the pleasure of creating
	Memory	
	Language and communication	
Social-emotional Area	Presentation	
	Activity	
	Leave-taking and relaxation	
	Board games	

DOG COOKIES

The objective of this game is that for RI to make some cookies for his friend.

We choose an inviting recipe, one appropriate for each RI. We lay out on a table all the ingredients, which can be labeled, in their proper quantities and the kitchen utensils needed for the preparation.

The RI will closely examine each ingredient: name, texture, odor, flavor...and then, the mixing begins!

Here's a simple recipe, with comments we can make about the ingredients:

- 1 natural yogurt. Calcium is good for the bones
- 1 cup of oat flakes. Oats are a good anti-oxidant
- 2 cups oatmeal flour
- 2 measures of brewer's yeast. Very good for the coat
- 1 1/2 cups of chicken broth. Source of animal protein
- 1 teaspoon chopped mint leaves for sweetening the breath

The mixture is formed into balls, which are placed on a baking tray. Cook at 180 °C in a pre-heated oven for 20 minutes.

Variations:

- Read the story "Dog Biscuit" by Helen Cooper, and use it to stimulate other activity: miming, questions and answers.

- When several days have passed, ask the RI to tell a story about the dogs and the cookies.

COMMANDS FOR THE DOG	MATERIALS
• Down • Stay • Carry • Mark • Treat 	• Ingredients for cookies • Mixing bowl • Yogurt serving cup (also used to measure) • Oven (responsibility of the therapist)

	Physical coordination	Objectives
Psychomotor Area	Sensory stimulation	• Exercise fine motor skills
	Space-time perception	• Exercise tactile perception
	Corporal awareness	• Exercise sense of taste
Cognitive Area	Atention and concentration	• Exercise sense of smell
	Recognition of categories	• Pay attention to instructions
	Memory	• Improve expression and verbal com munication
	Language and communication	• Learning good manners
Social-emotional Area	Presentation	• Stimulate teamwork
	Activity	• Experience the pleasure of laughter
	Leave-taking and relaxation	• Experience the pleasure of creating
	Board games	

The objective of this game is for the RI to recall an activity that he has done with his own hands.

We spread out a stretch of mural drawing paper and several plates with different colored finger paints. At the outset, the PT will go over with the RI the names of the colors and the other materials being used.

The RI decides which color to paint each of the dog's paws, while the dog remains in the "down" position. He paints the first paw, spreading the color gently over the paw pads with a brush. The dog then walks on the mural paper. That paw is then cleaned with a moist towel, and the instructions are repeated with each of the other three paws.

Once the dog is done with his part of the "painting," the RI leaves colored prints with his painted hands and feet. At this point the concepts of "left" and "right" can be taught.

Variations:

– We ask the RI to make a free drawing based on the dog. The dog is lying on a table near the RI, and the pencils have been placed beneath the dog's body. The RI must gently retrieve the pencils and, after using them, replace them, again gently, where they were.

COMMANDS FOR THE DOG	MATERIALS
• Down	• Mural paper
• Stay	• Finger paints
• Heel	• Plastic plates
	• Moist towelettes

	Physical coordination	Objectives
Psychomotor Area	Sensory stimulation	• Exercise concept of "right" and "left"
	Space-time perception	• Exercise fine motor skills
	Corporal awareness	• Exercise tactile perception
Cognitive Area	Atention and concentration	• Improve planning of tasks
	Recognition of categories	• Stimulate teamwork
	Memory	• Experience the pleasure of getting messy
	Language and communication	
Social-emotional Area	Presentation	
	Activity	
	Leave-taking and relaxation	
	Board games	

FEEDING

The object of this game is for the RI to prepare the dog's food and give it to him.

He must know, first of all, what utensils he needs to feed the dog and what steps he must follow.

We must keep in mind the following items:

- Each dog has a bowl of a specific shape and color.
- The dog must get a specific amount of food, measured in ounces or with different-sized containers. The PT will determine how many units of each measuring device are used.
- The dog's size must be determined (large or small) in order to relate it to the portion appropriate for its breed.

The following tasks are then performed:

- Find the dog's bowl: look for it around the room, following spatial instructions and distinguishing it from other bowls according to color and shape.
- Make a chart, with an appropriate degree of detail, showing what and how much the dog should eat
- Get the right food, identifying it by size, color, form and location.

The RI will make a list of steps using images, written words and his memory.

- Have the utensils ready
- Tell the dog to sit and stay (waiting time)
- Put the food in the bowl
- Place the bowl on the floor
- Tell the dog to go to the bowl
- Let him eat by himself, or feed him with a spoon.

COMMANDS FOR THE DOG	MATERIALS
• Sit	• Plates
• Stay	• Quality dog food
• Come	• Measuring vessels
• Treat	• Scale

	Physical coordination	Objectives
Psychomotor Area	Sensory stimulation	• Exercise hand-eye coordination
	Space-time perception	• Exercise tactile perception and sense of smell
	Corporal awareness	• Exercise sense of spatial relationship to other objects
Cognitive Area	Atention and concentration	• Develop task-fulfillment skills
	Recognition of categories	• Acquire or exercise nation of correct number and quantity
	Memory	• Acquire or exercise notion of single or multiple units
	Language and communication	• Visually recognize numbers
Social-emotional Area	Presentation	• Develop logical-mathematical thought
	Activity	• Develop logical reasoning skills
	Leave-taking and relaxation	• Experience the pleasure of completing a task
	Board games	

THE DETECTIVE'S SHEET

The objective of this game is for the RI to guess, by name, which dog is hidden under a sheet.

The IP and his dogs take their places in front of the RI, and the IP introduces the animals one by one. He asks questions about the visible differences between the animals, and emphasizes them by repetition.

With the RI's back turned, the IP will place a sheet over one of the dogs and escort the others out of the room.

The RI takes a seat beside the covered dog and asks the IP questions in order to discover the hidden dog's identity. The IP can only respond "yes" or "no."

To enhance interaction with the animal, the RI is allowed to touch the dog beneath the sheet while formulating his questions.

Variations:

– We can hide the dog inside a travel crate so as to more markedly separate it from the RI.

– We can bring body parts into the game: the RI must guess, by way of feeling with his hand, what part of the dog's body he is touching under the sheet.

COMMANDS FOR THE DOG	MATERIALS
• Stay • Down • Bang 	• Traveling crate • Sheet

		Objectives
Psychomotor Area	Physical coordination	• Making a mental image of a body
	Sensory stimulation	• Develop or evaluate visual memory
	Space-time perception	• Develop or evaluate short-term memory
	Corporal awareness	• Distinguish among parts of a whole
Cognitive Area	Atention and concentration	• Acknowledge presence or absence of things or individuals
	Recognition of categories	• Enrich vocabulary
	Memory	• Develop logical thinking
	Language and communication	• Learn the dogs' names
Social-emotional Area	Presentation	• Accept rules of social interaction
	Activity	• Stimulate active listening
	Leave-taking and relaxation	
	Board games	

The object of this game is to promote visual contact between the RI and the dog.

At first, we want to encourage the RI's overall visual contact with the animal. We escort the RI to a particular place in the room and we ask him:

- to observe the dog each time the animal sits. If it will not disrupt the activity, the dog can bark to attract the RI's attention or the IP can make a pre-determined noise.
- to observe the dog while the animal moves around the room, either crawling, on four legs or on two legs.
- to keep his eyes fixed on the dog while the animal approaches him head-on.
- to keep his eyes fixed on a certain point of the dog's body (identified with an adhesive label) while the dog does a trick.
- to keep sustained visual contact with the dog while giving him a treat.

Variations:

- Go through the above-mentioned steps, with the RI in movement instead of the dog.

- Go through the above-mentioned steps with both the RI and the dog in movement.

Visual contact and greeting:

The objective is for two RIs to greet each other, looking at each other eyes while shaking hands.

Each one has an adhesive label affixed to the midpoint of the brow. We have the dog sit between them. When they shake hands, we place two treats between them, which will be divided between them and given to the dog, though each RI's eyes must remain on the label on his partner's brow.

COMMANDS FOR THE DOG	MATERIALS
• Paw	• Treats
• Sit	• Adhesive labels
• Get it	• Rattle
• Crawl	
• Back	
• Stay	

SENSORIAL STIMULATION

	Physical coordination	Objectives
Psychomotor Area	Sensory stimulation	• Exercise hand-eye coordination
	Space-time perception	• Exercise visual perception of spatial relationships
	Corporal awareness	• Accept rules for social interaction
Cognitive Area	Atention and concentration	• Develop capacity for observation
	Recognition of categories	
	Memory	
	Language and communication	
Social-emotional Area	Presentation	
	Activity	
	Leave-taking and relaxation	
	Board games	

The object of the game is for the individual to get closer to the dog, motivated by the prospect of feeding him.

On one side, we have the dog in "stay" position and, on the other, a certain distance away, is the RI with a bowl containing dog food. Between the two, at varying intervals, are three different colored bowls.

The therapist or the RI asks the dog how many treats he wants. The number of barks is the number of spoonfuls to be placed in the first bowl.

Once he has placed the correct amount of food in the bowl, the RI returns to his position and the dog advances to eat what is in that bowl.

The question is repeated and, depending on the willingness of the RI, he will go through the same steps with the second and third bowls. At a later stage, the dog will remain in one place throughout the exercise.

The RI will take each successive bowl containing food to the animal and return to his place.

Variations:

These can be done once the RI is comfortable taking all three plates to the dog.

– The bowl to be taken to the dog is determined by a colored roulette wheel.

– Bowls representing the day's three main meals will be situated along a time-line, providing the opportunity to work with and ask questions about the relationship between eating habits and daily routines.

– The number of treats or handfuls of food to be placed in the bowls can be used as a variable.

COMMANDS FOR THE DOG	MATERIALS
• Sit • Stay • Eat • Spot ✍	• Dog bowls of different colors • Dog food or treats • Colored roulette wheel • Illustrations of the day's three main meals

		Objectives
Psychomotor Area	Physical coordination	• Reduce stress
	Sensory stimulation	• Exercise hand-eye coordination
	Space-time perception	• Develop visual contact
	Corporal awareness	• Enhance self-esteem
Cognitive Area	Atention and concentration	• Exercise fine motor skills
	Recognition of categories	• Acquire or exercise notion of correct numbers and quantity
	Memory	• Exercise sense of timing
	Language and communication	• Put eating habits in context of daily routine
Social-emotional Area	Presentation	
	Activity	
	Leave-taking and relaxation	
	Board games	

The objective of this game is to imitate the form and movements of various animals.

We lay out on a table, face down, cards with illustrations of various animals. The RI tosses a large die and the dog retrieves it, showing the number that came up.

The RI counts out that number on the arrayed cards, turns over the one corresponding to his number and says the name of the animal out loud. The RI then imitates the form and movements of that animal for the dog, which will then do his own version of the imitation.

With the dog attentively observing, the RI acts out a representation of the animal. For example:

- Giraffe: stand up straight and stretch so as to appear very tall
- Snake: slither along the floor
- Crab: walk backward
- Dolphin: jump through a hoop
- Lion: open the mouth wide as if roaring, shake hair like a mane
- Bear: Walk with forearms suspended out front

Variations:

- The RI spins a roulette Wheel and imitates, in as detailed a fashion as possible, the animal that comes up. The dog, after observing, picks out the card with the illustration of that animal.

COMMANDS FOR THE DOG	MATERIALS
• Stand	• Cards showing animals
• Stay	• Cards showing movements
• Jump	• Animal roulette wheel
• Beg	
• Back	
• Sit	
• Get it	
• Crawl	
• Fetch	

		Objectives
Psychomotor Area	Physical coordination	• Stimulate the imagination
	Sensory stimulation	• Stimulate creativity: thinking out side the box
	Space-time perception	• Acquire or exercise capacity to use symbols
	Corporal awareness	• Acquire or exercise capacity for imitation
Cognitive Area	Atention and concentration	• Exercise balance
	Recognition of categories	• Acquire or exercise notion of correct numbers and quantity
	Memory	• Stimulate physical interaction and physical contact
	Language and communication	• Experience the pleasure of laughter
Social-emotional Area	Presentation	• Explore different kinds of communication: mime, rhythm, figurative, theatrical
	Activity	
	Leave-taking and relaxation	
	Board games	

WHAT FOR?

The object of this game is for the RI to identify the function of different parts of the dog's body and relate them to his own body parts and functions.

The dog is lying on the floor next to the RI. We begin slowly, touching the different parts of the dog's body.

We pay special attention to the way in which we caress and touch the dog, reminding the RI that it must be done gently.

When we touch a part of the body, we say its name, talk about its function and draw a parallel to the parts of our own body.

It soon becomes obvious that the dog has a body part that we do not: the tail. This provides the chance to joke around, exercise our wit and laugh, and it also gives us ample opportunity to talk about the tail's function.

Variations:

– The IP says a bodily function and the RI touches and names the body part that carries it out.

– Making pairs: The dog gives the RI a card showing a part of the body and the RI then must find the card that illustrates the corresponding function. For each successful pairing of cards, the dog will do a trick at the RI's command.

– The dog wears some clips on different parts of his body. The RI must choose the card that illustrates the function corresponding the location of each clip.

COMMANDS FOR THE DOG	MATERIALS
• Stay	• Cards with body parts
• Down	• Cards with movements
• Drop	• Cards with functions
• Carry	• Clips
• Various tricks	• Treats

		Objectives
Psychomotor Area	Physical coordination	• Exercise hand-eye coordination
	Sensory stimulation	• Develop sense of anatomy
	Space-time perception	• Recognize traits and functions
	Corporal awareness	• Recognize parts of a whole
Cognitive Area	Atention and concentration	• Develop symbolic thinking
	Recognition of categories	• Stimulate the imagination
	Memory	• Enrich vocabulary
	Language and communication	• Accept rules for social interaction
Social-emotional Area	Presentation	• Stimulate active listening
	Activity	
	Leave-taking and relaxation	
	Board games	

The objective of this game is for the RI to carry out, alongside the dog, a series of actions as part of a circuit.

The activity takes place along a course defined with objects (cones, stools, boxes...). At each one, the RI stops and carries out a certain action with the dog.

The technician and the dog first go along the circuit performing each action. The RI must pay close attention in order to be able to repeat the circuit, with or without help as the case may be.

Here are some suggestions for tasks:

– At each "stop," the RI must touch a certain part of the dog's body: head, belly, tail, leg, rump, snout, withers, fetlock.
– Place a treat in spatial relation to an object: beneath, on top of, in front of, behind.
– Pick up, or place, at each "stop" a certain number of treats, and give them to the dog.
– Carry out an action or task: brush, hug, feed, kiss.
– Place a certain colored hoop or handkerchief around the dog's neck
– Give the dog a command, either easy or difficult: "sit," "paw," "down".

Some of these tasks or actions can be combined, allowing the RI to exercise his creativity.

COMMANDS FOR THE DOG	MATERIALS
• Sit	• Objects for establishing the circuit
• Stand	• Elements needed for each task
• Stay	or action
• Treat	
• Related tricks	

		Objectives
Psychomotor Area	Physical coordination	• Develop sense of anatomy
	Sensory stimulation	• Acquire or exercise notions of space and direction
	Space-time perception	• Pay attention to movements of others
	Corporal awareness	• Acquire or exercise the ability to imitate
Cognitive Area	Atention and concentration	• Develop or evaluate visual memory
	Recognition of categories	• Develop capacity for observation
	Memory	• Learn and respect social norms
	Language and communication	• Association: Stimulate group cooperation
Social-emotional Area	Presentation	• Experience the pleasure of sense of achievement
	Activity	• Stimulate the imagination
	Leave-taking and relaxation	
	Board games	

The objective is for the RI and the dog to guess where the dog's treat is hidden.

The IP introduces the game. He takes a treat and, keeping his hands in plain sight, encloses the treat in the palm of one.

The RI touches or blows on the hand he thinks holds the treat. If he is right, he gets to give the dog the treat, and the dog does a "happy" trick.

Then the IP gives the dog a chance to guess. The dog touches one of the IP's hands with his paw. If he guesses correctly, the RI congratulates him. If the choice was wrong, the RI encourages the dog to try again, or consoles him by saying he'll get another chance later.

At a later stage, it is the RI who hides the treat in his hand. The dog "guesses" by touching a hand with either his paw or snout. Also, the dog can hide the treats under his body and it is the RI who must find them, by feeling.

Variations:

– We place containers of differing color and size upside-down on a low table. Taking turns, the RI and the dog must guess which one covers a hidden treat. They both observe the proceedings attentively as a team, helping each other out, one blowing or touching and the other signaling with paw or snout until they determine which one hides the treat.

COMMANDS FOR THE DOG	MATERIALS
• Sit	• Treats
• Mark	• Chairs
• Treat	• Containers
	• Low table

	Physical coordination	Objectives
Psychomotor Area	Sensory stimulation	• Develop observation skills
	Space-time perception	• Strengthen affective ties
	Corporal awareness	• Accept challenges
Cognitive Area	Atention and concentration	• Learn to handle frustration
	Recognition of categories	• Respect waiting times and turns
	Memory	• Cooperation: Stimulate relationships of mutual help
	Language and communication	• Stimulate trust in others
Social-emotional Area	Presentation	
	Activity	
	Leave-taking and relaxation	
	Board games	

HIDE THE TREATS

The objective of this game is for the RI to find treats hidden on the dog's body.

The dog lies on a table or the floor or the ground, whichever position affords the RI the easiest access to its body.

The RI closes his eyes while the IP hides treats on or under parts of the dog's body; in the fur, under the legs, the tail, the belly, or behind the collar. Then, with his eyes open, the RI searches for the treats by sense of touch.

When he finds one, he can either give it immediately to the dog or save it in a bowl to be given later.

Variations:

– The searching can be done with eyes closed or blindfolded.

– The search proceeds by body parts, which are indicated by the therapist by way of the die or by showing a card.

– Introduce the concept of "cold" and "hot."

– Draw a parallel between the part of the dog's body where the treat was found and the corresponding part of the RI's body, using adhesive labels. Point out the differences, such as the fact that the RI does not have a tail.

– The "found" treats can be used in talking about numbers and for doing simple arithmetic.

COMMANDS FOR THE DOG	MATERIALS
• Down	• Treats
• Stay	• Adhesive labels
• Yuck	• Cards showing body parts
• Treat	• Body-part die
	• Dog collar
	• Bowl for treats

		Objectives
Psychomotor Area	Physical coordination	• Exercise sense of touch
	Sensory stimulation	• Enhance bond between the RI and the dog
	Space-time perception	• Exercise dexterity
	Corporal awareness	• Develop awareness of anatomy
Cognitive Area	Atention and concentration	• Develop or evaluate short-term memory
	Recognition of categories	• Develop or evaluate awareness of own body
	Memory	
	Language and communication	
Social-emotional Area	Presentation	
	Activity	
	Leave-taking and relaxation	
	Board games	

The objective of this activity is that the RI brush and preen the entire dog by himself.

The dog is in a comfortable position that is reassuring to the RI. This can mean either standing or lying down on the ground or on a table, but necessarily calm and still.

Before beginning, we explain why the dog needs to be brushed regularly and we relate it to a person's routine of daily hygiene. This can be done either with natural and spontaneous conversation or with the aid of illustrative cards.

We show the RI the tools used for brushing, allowing him to examine and touch them. He can choose the one he likes best from the basket of brushes. The RI runs his fingers through the dog's coat to determine the kind of brushing to be performed. We explain that brushing can be done with the direction of the hair growth or against the direction of growth. We can use the profile of the RI's face to illustrate this point, lightly tracing it downward with a fingertip to illustrate the "with the direction" brushing and tracing it upward for the "against the direction".

Then the RI holds the brush in one hand while resting the other on the dog. He then preens the various parts of the dog's body.

The IP tells the RI about the sensations the dog is feeling depending on the area being brushed and the skill level of the brusher. This portion can also serve as a review of the names of body parts.

Variations:

- A picture of a brush is shown, and either the RI or the dog then selects that brush from the basket.

- A brush is described verbally and the RI selects the correct one.

- The body-part die is tossed, and the body part that comes up is the one to be brushed.

COMMANDS FOR THE DOG	MATERIALS
• Down • Sit • Fetch	• Different types of brush • Materials to adapt the brushes to the RI's capabilities

	Physical coordination	Objectives
Psychomotor Area	Sensory stimulation	• Learning to brush the dog
	Space-time perception	• Develop concept of anatomy
	Corporal awareness	• Exercise fine motor skills
Cognitive Area	Atention and concentration	• Exercise sense of touch
	Recognition of categories	• Improve task planning
	Memory	
	Language and communication	
Social-emotional Area	Presentation	
	Activity	
	Leave-taking and relaxation	
	Board games	

The objective of this game is for the RI to carry out pre-established actions at specific points on a circuit.

We place four cones on the ground in a square. On each one of them there is a piece of paper with an instruction. Once he has memorized the instructions, the RI will perform a full passage along the circuit without the help of the IP to the degree that is possible.

Here are some actions that can be carried out at each point in the circuit:

- Touch a certain part of the dog; head, belly, withers, snout, etc.
- Perform a certain action with the dog; caress, brush, kiss, hug.
- Command the dog to do a trick, either deciding spontaneously or using the trick die.
- Do anything that comes to mind.
- Imitate the animal signaled by the dog.
- A combination of the above actions

The RI will make the circuit with the dog at differing speeds and without the aid of the IP in order to improve his memory skills.

COMMANDS FOR THE DOG

- Stay
- Heel

MATERIALS

- Cones
- Cards showing skills
- Brushes
- Food bowl
- Water bowl
- Trick die

		Objectives
Psychomotor Area	Physical coordination	• Improve overall dynamic coordination
	Sensory stimulation	• Develop sense of anatomy
	Space-time perception	• Regulate tone of voice
	Corporal awareness	• Acquire or exercise ability to imitate
Cognitive Area	Atention and concentration	• Stimulate the imagination
	Recognition of categories	• Enrich vocabulary
	Memory	• Practice reading
	Language and communication	• Improve task planning skills
Social-emotional Area	Presentation	• Experience the pleasure of achievement
	Activity	
	Leave-taking and relaxation	
	Board games	

SENSORY PETTING

The objective of this game is for the RI, using the sense of touch, to more completely perceive the sensations the dog provides him, and in so doing become more comfortable with him.

We put the dog in a position that encourages the RI to come closer, and we help the RI express his affection by way of petting.

At first, we observe the different parts of the dog's body and we compare them with our own body.

Then we place the hands of the RI on different parts of the dog's body to enhance distinct tactile sensations; such as those of texture, temperature, etc.

As the RI makes these discoveries, with or without our help, we encourage him to talk about his feelings:

– Softness: the dog's coat, the difference between the fur on the ears and on the tail.
– Roughness: the paw pads.
– Wetness: the nose.
– Warmth: the belly.
– Feel the beating of the heart.

Variations:

– After a good rapport has been established between the RI and the dog, we can cover the RI's eyes and hold his hand on a certain part of the dog's body. He must determine solely by touch which part it is.

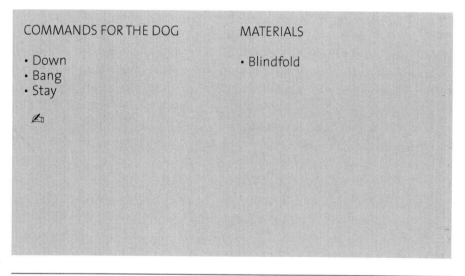

COMMANDS FOR THE DOG	MATERIALS
• Down	• Blindfold
• Bang	
• Stay	

SENSORIAL STIMULATION

		Objectives
Psychomotor Area	Physical coordination	**Objectives**
	Sensory stimulation	• Exercise senses of touch and smell
	Space-time perception	• Exercise hearing and distinguishing between sounds
	Corporal awareness	• Develop sense of anatomy
Cognitive Area	Atention and concentration	• Develop and control muscle strength
	Recognition of categories	• Establish affinities between objects
		• Recognize parts of a whole
	Memory	• Develop observation skills
	Language and communication	• Enhance recognition by touch
Social-emotional Area	Presentation	• Create a welcoming and anxiety-free environment
	Activity	
	Leave-taking and relaxation	
	Board games	

The objective of this game is for the individual to perform a manual task along with the dog.

The dog lies calmly on a table. The RI is seated in front of him.

Hidden in the dog's coat are several pencils that the RI will use to draw with. When he finishes using one pencil, before finding another he must replace the one he has used where he found it.

He can make a drawing:

– of whatever he wants to
– of himself with the dog
– of his family with its pets
– of a dog, connecting dots already on the sheet of paper

Variations:

– The RI colors a drawing of a dog. We place different colored pencils under the dog's different body parts. The therapist tosses the body-parts die and, depending what comes up, the RI removes the pencil from beneath that part and uses it to color.

COMMANDS FOR THE DOG	MATERIALS
• Down • Stay	• Paper • Colored pencils • Body-parts die

	Physical coordination	Objectives
Psychomotor Area	Sensory stimulation	• Exercise fine motor skills • Enhance self-esteem • Recognize parts of a whole • Express feelings: sadness, happiness, anger • Improve oral comprehension • Encourage socialization • Encourage group interaction and communication • Exercise sense of touch
	Space-time perception	
	Corporal awareness	
Cognitive Area	Atention and concentration	
	Recognition of categories	
	Memory	
	Language and communication	
Social-emotional Area	Presentation	
	Activity	
	Leave-taking and relaxation	
	Board games	

MUSICAL HOOPS

The object of this game is for the RI to acknowledge the cessation of auditory stimulus and to follow the instructions of the IP.

We place different colored cones on the floor around the room without apparent order. Then we give the RI a colored hoop. While the music is playing, the RI walks freely around the room with the dog. But when the music stops, he must quickly place the hoop on the same-colored cone, all the time accompanied by the dog.

We can encourage a little stress-free competition among the RIs , seeing who is the fastest in placing the hoop on the right cone. The winner finds a treat under the cone, and gives it to his dog. If the dog is trained in placing hoops on cones, this variation can be introduced to the game. The RI guides him to the right cone.

If there is only one dog available, the first among the RIs who correctly places his hoop gets to be accompanied by the dog, holding his leash, in the following game.

Variations:

– The cones can stand for a mathematical result. The therapist poses an operation of arithmetic and the RI must place the hoop on the right cone according the correct result.

– Find an object that "goes with" one being held by the RI under one of the cones (e.g. the RI has a fork, and must find the knife).

– Each time the music stops, he hugs another participant

COMMANDS FOR THE DOG	MATERIALS
• Carry	• Hoops
• Heel	• Cone
• Put hoop	• Music

		Objectives
Psychomotor Area	Physical coordination	• Exercise auditory perception and rhythm • Acquire or exercise notions of space and direction • Following instructions • Improve oral comprehension • Acquire or exercise concept of colors • Experience the pleasure of achievement • Stimulate active listening • Work with mathematical concepts
	Sensory stimulation	
	Space-time perception	
	Corporal awareness	
Cognitive Area	Atention and concentration	
	Recognition of categories	
	Memory	
	Language and communication	
Social-emotional Area	Presentation	
	Activity	
	Leave-taking and relaxation	
	Board games	

"ROW, ROW, ROW YOUR BOAT..."

The objective of this game is for the RI to get used to contact with the dog and that he interact with him, following the IP's instructions.

The dog is lying down, with his hindquarters as close to the RI as possible.

We encourage the RI to move his hands toward the dog's coat, and then rest them there.

If the RI feels too anxious, we proceed more slowly with the approach process, assuring him that the dog is is friend. When he is calm and confident enough to be next to the animal, we continue the activity.

When a children's song like the one that gives the title to this exercise is played, the RI strokes the dog's back, pats him softly, scratches him gently or simply keeps his hand resting on the dog. When the song is over or is interrupted, the RI performs an action previously agreed upon, such as:

– Place a hoop around the dog's head.
– Give the dog a treat
– Collect treats in a container to give him later.
– Place an adhesive label or a clip on a certain part of the dog.

If the RI stops petting the dog while the music is playing, he must then perform a task, for example:

– make a complete circle around the animal
– perform the movement indicated by the dog using the "movements" cards

COMMANDS FOR THE DOG	MATERIALS
• Down	• Movements cards
• Stay	• Treats
	• Bowl
	• Hoops
	• Clips

68

		Objectives
Psychomotor Area	Physical coordination	• Build trust in the therapy dog
	Sensory stimulation	• Increase self-esteem
	Space-time perception	• Exercise fine motor skills
	Corporal awareness	• Exercise auditory perception and rhythm
Cognitive Area	Atention and concentration	• Develop and control muscular strength
	Recognition of categories	• Follow instructions
	Memory	• Experience the pleasure of achievement
	Language and communication	• Improve short-term memory
Social-emotional Area	Presentation	
	Activity	
	Leave-taking and relaxation	
	Board games	

PIN THE TAIL ON THE DOG

This game is like "Pin the tail on the donkey," only it's "Pin the tail on the dog."

To "earn" the tail, the RI must take the ball that the dog brings him in his mouth. Then, following the therapist's instructions, he throws it into a basket

- the same color as the ball
- a different color from the ball
- labeled with a certain number
- has a certain geometric shape
- that represents the answer to a riddle

He then tells the dog to fetch the ball, but the dog brings him instead a tail that the RI will now pin on the drawing of a dog. With his eyes closed, the RI walks beside the dog along a relatively difficult circuit to reach the board where the drawing is affixed, and he pins it on.

Variations:

- We can affix to the walls drawings or photographs of dogs from breeds different from the one in the tail-pinning image. The tails of those dogs are placed in a basket. The dog takes the RI the tails one at a time, and he must affix them on the correct dog.

COMMANDS FOR THE DOG	MATERIALS
• Sit	• Colored balls
• Stay	• Baskets
• Give	• Illustrations of dogs without tails
• Carry	• Tails
• Stand	• Blindfold
• Get it	

SENSORIAL STIMULATION

	Physical coordination	Objectives
Psychomotor Area	Sensory stimulation	• Exercise gross motor skills
	Space-time perception	• Exercise fine motor skills
	Corporal awareness	• Acquire or exercise notion of color
		• Acquire or exercise notion of size
Cognitive Area	Atention and concentration	• Acquire or exercise notion of shape
	Recognition of categories	• Stimulate active listening
	Memory	• Association: Stimulate group cooperation
	Language and communication	• Experience the pleasure of achievement
Social-emotional Area	Presentation	• Experience the pleasure of guessing correctly
	Activity	
	Leave-taking and relaxation	
	Board games	

The objective of this game is for the RI to identify where sounds are coming from.

We place the RI, either blindfolded or with his eyes closed, at a certain point in the room. The dog roams around, barking on a signal from the therapist or technician. Each time the dog barks, the RI must point to where the sound is coming from.

When he has done so correctly, the dog goes over to him to receive either a treat or a congratulatory pat.

Variations:

– We show the RI cards illustrating dogs in different emotional states. Once the situations are understood, we play a recording of various canine vocalizations and he matches them with the correct card.

– A game of "catch" with a musical ball. The RI rolls a musical ball along the floor toward the dog. The dog takes it in his mouth, and sends it back to the RI, who, with his eyes closed, must "catch" it in his hands.

– If we have more than one dog, we line them up behind the RI and have them bark one by one. The RI must say which dog each bark belongs to.

COMMANDS FOR THE DOG	MATERIALS
• Speak	• Musical ball
• Drop	• Blindfold
• Fetch	• Illustrations of dogs in various
• Stay	emotional states
• Sit	
• Get it	

	Physical coordination	Objectives
Psychomotor Area	Sensory stimulation	• Exercise auditory perception and rhythm
	Space-time perception	• Exercise gross motor skills
	Corporal awareness	• Exercise fine motor skills
Cognitive Area	Atention and concentration	• Exercise distinguishing between sounds
	Recognition of categories	• Exercise sense of spatial orientation
	Memory	• Exercise sense of timing and sequence
	Language and communication	• Stimulate physical interaction and physical contact
Social-emotional Area	Presentation	• Listening
	Activity	• Explore different ways of communicating
	Leave-taking and relaxation	
	Board games	

HUNTING FOR MUSHROOMS

We place different colored stylized mushrooms around the floor. Underneath each one, we put materials the RI's will work with.

Taking turns, each participant spins the roulette wheel or tosses a colored die He then walks a route defined by the mushrooms of the color that came up, either in a pre-determined order or at random, though in both cases avoiding those of another color. He completes this circuit with the dog. At the first mushroom, the dog sits to await whatever instructions the RI will give him.

Under each mushroom there are things for people or for dogs. The RI must perform the appropriate action with each tool. For example:

- Dog brush. Brush the dog.
- Human brush or comb. Comb his hair.
- Dog bowl and food. Feed the dog.
- Plate and silverware. Set the table.
- Water bowl and water. Give the dog water.
- Glass and bottle of water. Drink.
- Dog shampoo. Wash the dog.
- Shower gel and sponge. Act out taking a shower.

Variations:

- Under every mushroom there is a card. The RI must ask the dog to bring him the tools needed to perform the action illusted on the card.

COMMANDS FOR THE DOG	MATERIALS
• Stay	• Mushrooms of various colors
• Stand	• Dog grooming materials
• Fetch	• Human hygiene materials
• Together	• Dog toys
• Sit	• Human toys
• Find	• Colored roulette wheel or die
	• Cards illustrating different actions

74

		Objectives
Psychomotor Area	Physical coordination	• Exercise fine motor skills • Learn companions' names • Exercise hand-eye coordination • Exercise visual perception • Pay attention to movements of others • Enhance language use: expression and comprehension • Develop social interaction • Develop concept of fairness, giving each participant the same amount of time • Learning and following rules
	Sensory stimulation	
	Space-time perception	
	Corporal awareness	
Cognitive Area	Atention and concentration	
	Recognition of categories	
	Memory	
	Language and communication	
Social-emotional Area	Presentation	
	Activity	
	Leave-taking and relaxation	
	Board games	

The objective of this game is for the RI to gain enough trust in the dog and confidence in himself to be able to feed the animal in a calm, orderly and precise fashion.

Giving the dog a treat can be a challenge for the RI, and sometimes requires a certain amount of work. This process must be carried out gradually but confidently, with all actions intended to increase the self-esteem of the RI and his trust in the dog.

The dog is in the "sit" position a certain distance from the RI. We give a treat to the RI to see if he is willing to give it to the dog. From here on, we are guided principally by the degree of willingness of the RI.

Depending on the state of mind of the RI, we choose the next step:

1- The RI can toss the dog the treat, and the dog eats it off the floor.

2- He can use something on which to offer the dog the treat. This could be the palm of the IP's hand or a plate, tray, etc.

  – The RI places the treat on the IP's palm. The IP then gives the treat to the dog while saying clearly and slowly how much the dog likes getting treats.
  – The RI places the treat on the IP's palm, then uses his own hand to move the IP's hand to the dog's mouth.
  – The IP holds his hand below the dog's mouth. The RI places the treat on the hand, and the dog eats it.

COMMANDS FOR THE DOG	MATERIALS
• Sit	• Treats
• Stay	• Plate or tray
• Beg	
• Treat	

	Physical coordination	Objectives
Psychomotor Area	Sensory stimulation	• Exercise gross motor skills
	Space-time perception	• Exercise hand-eye coordination
	Corporal awareness	• Exercise sense of touch
Cognitive Area	Atention and concentration	• Exercise sense of smell
	Recognition of categories	• Acquire or exercise notion of number and quantity
	Memory	• Decrease over-sensitivity
	Language and communication	• Increase self-esteem
Social-emotional Area	Presentation	• Experience the sensation of achievement
	Activity	
	Leave-taking and relaxation	
	Board games	

The object of the game is for the RI to give the dog his treats more directly, actually touching him.

We follow the same procedure as with the Distance Treats, gradually decreasing the space separating the RI and the dog.

The treats can be given:

1- On the palm of the RI's hand, with or without the help of the IP.
2- Using other parts of the RI's body; leg, arm, etc.
3- With a utensil: a spoon, tongs, etc.
4- Making a "tong" together with the IP's hand

The RI might find direct contact with the dog's saliva unpleasant. This is something to keep in mind, and must be dealt with in a manner that allows the therapy to continue.

Variations:

- The treat-giving can be done before or after another activity, or as an activity in itself.

- The idea of order and numbers can be introduced by establishing a certain amount of treats to be given.

- We can ask the RI to observe where we hide the treat, and have him find it

COMMANDS FOR THE DOG	MATERIALS
• Sit	• Treats
• Treat	• Shakers
• Mark	
• Stay	

		Objectives
Psychomotor Area	Physical coordination	• Exercise fine motor skills
	Sensory stimulation	• Exercise hand-eye coordination
	Space-time perception	• Acquire or exercise notion of numbers and quantity
	Corporal awareness	• Acquire or exercise notion of color
Cognitive Area	Atention and concentration	• Experience the pleasure of achievement
	Recognition of categories	• Experience the pleasure of guessing correctly
	Memory	• Decrease over-sensitivity
	Language and communication	• Patience
Social-emotional Area	Presentation	
	Activity	
	Leave-taking and relaxation	
	Board games	

The objective of this game is for the RI to express his preference for the way he should be congratulated for completing a task or performing an action correctly.

Depending on the RI's degree of willingness and state of mind, the IP situates the dog on the floor or on a table in the "down" position. The RI and the IP take their places next to him in a way that encourages contact and sets the stage for a conversation.

The IP starts talking about good and positive and pleasant things the dog does every day (illustrative cards can be used if so desired), and he asks the RI how he thinks the dog likes to be rewarded or congratulated for what he does.

- By spoken word
- By being petted
- With his favorite toy
- With a sound associated with food (clicker)
- With food

While this is going on, the dog remains lying down and receives petting and expressions of affection from the RI. At a certain point, with or without prompting by the IP, the person or people talk about the ways in which they like to be rewarded or congratulated.

Now the talk is transferred into the practical realm. Each time the dog performs a trick or completes an action correctly, the RI rewards him. The same occurs when the RI completes a task or demonstrates a skill: his companions or the IP will praise or congratulate him in the way he likes best or in the manner deemed most appropriate.

Variations:

- This same exercise can be used to work on ways to discourage certain behaviors or actions. We can talk about the way the dog might want to be "corrected" by the IP when he does something wrong. The RIs are then invited to express their opinions on the matter.

COMMANDS FOR THE DOG	MATERIALS
• Down	• Cards illustrating actions
• Stay	• Skills cards
• Tricks	• Treats
	• Clicker

SENSORIAL STIMULATION

	Physical coordination	Objectives
Psychomotor Area	Sensory stimulation	• Express feelings: sadness, happiness, anger
	Space-time perception	• Articulate fantasies
	Corporal awareness	• Express personality
Cognitive Area	Atention and concentration	• Listening without interrupting, taking turns
	Recognition of categories	• Experience the shedding of inhibitions
	Memory	
	Language and communication	
Social-emotional Area	Presentation	
	Activity	
	Leave-taking and relaxation	
	Board games	

The objective is for the RI to identify objects by way of photographs, and then put them to use correctly.

We have two boxes. One contains things we're going to work with, and the other contains pictures of those same objects.

The dog takes a photo from the box and gives it to the RI, who observes, names and describes the pictured object. Then the RI, with eyes open or shut, reaches into the other box and, by feeling, finds the object in the photo.

If he withdraws the correct object, he can then use it to interact with the dog.

If it is not the right object, he gives it to the dog, who puts it back in the box.

Variations:

– Match the photos with the outline of their corresponding objects. If the match is correct, the RI gets to use the object itself to interact with the dog.

– Near the end of the sesión, the RI recalls the objects he has used and for each correct one mentioned the dog gets a treat.

– The dog takes the RI an item from daily life. The RI describes it and uses it in a way that demonstrates its function to the dog.

COMMANDS FOR THE DOG	MATERIALS
• Fetch • Drop	• Boxes • Physical objects (tools, etc.) • Photos of those objects

		Objectives
Psychomotor Area	Physical coordination	• Identifying objects
	Sensory stimulation	• Exercise sense of touch
	Space-time perception	• Acquire or exercise symbolic thinking
	Corporal awareness	• Relate objects to one another
Cognitive Area	Atention and concentration	• Recognize properties and functions of objects
	Recognition of categories	• Stimulate the imagination
	Memory	
	Language and communication	
Social-emotional Area	Presentation	
	Activity	
	Leave-taking and relaxation	
	Board games	

83

The objective of the game is for the RI to match pairs of objects according to indications from the IP.

The session begins with the dog taking a basket of objects to the RI and showing him what's inside (pairs of objects that share the same function but differ in size, shape or color). The objects are examined by both the dog and the RI with the latter commenting on them, possibly with encouragement or prompting from the IP.

Then the items are separated, with one of each pair being deposited in another basket.

The dog selects an object from the second basket and takes it to the RI, who, with his eyes closed, must reach into his basket and find the object that forms the pair.

Once he has matched all the pairs, the RI explains to the dog, which is seated by his side, everything he knows about the object and the manner in which it is employed.

Variations:

– The RI can match the objects with all of them arrayed and in sight.

– The RI can match the objects without having previously examined them.

– The RI can match the objects that have the same function but that differ in shape.

– Roles can be switched. The RI shows an object to the dog, who then finds the matching item.

COMMANDS FOR THE DOG	MATERIALS
• Sit	• Pairs of various objects
• Down	• Baskets
• Stay	
• Fetch	
• Drop	
• Give	
• Carry	

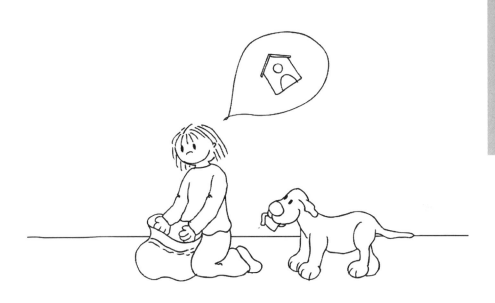

		Objectives
Psychomotor Area	Physical coordination	• Acquire or exercise the capacity to concentrate
	Sensory stimulation	• Acquire or exercise notions of size, shape and texture
	Space-time perception	• Work with daily activities or routines
	Corporal awareness	• Emphasize the visual following an object from place to place
Cognitive Area	Atention and concentration	• Improve language comprehension and expression
	Recognition of categories	• Enrich vocabulary
	Memory	
	Language and communication	
Social-emotional Area	Presentation	
	Activity	
	Leave-taking and relaxation	
	Board games	

85

The objective of the game is for the RI to roll around on surfaces of differing textures.

The RI is shown how the dog rolls upon hearing the command, "Roll over." Then the RI is taught how to impart the command so that the dog obeys.

After the RI has commanded the dog to roll over on several surfaces (grass, a mat, sand, clay...), the roles are reversed and the dog gets to give the orders. The dog sits or stands on the surface he wants the RI to roll on. At his bark, the RI must roll over the number of times required by the dog.

The number of rolls is determined by:

− the number of barks
− the number that comes up on a die toss
− continues until the IP or dog gives a signal to stop, or until the RI covers the ground to the point where the dog is waiting in the "down" position.

When both the RI and the dog have rolled on the various surfaces, they will have a race, with both of them rolling across a selected surface to a finish line.

COMMANDS FOR THE DOG

• Roll over
• Sit
• Down
• Speak

MATERIALS

• Surfaces of differing texture
• Numbered die
• Card illustrating "roll over" trick

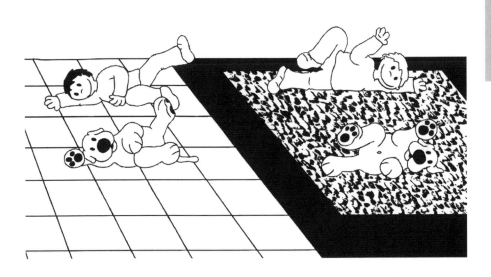

		Objectives
Psychomotor Area	Physical coordination	• Exercise gross motor skills • Exercise sensory perception • Exercise sense of place in space • Exercise balance • Imitate movements: body control and command • Pay attention to movements of others • Acquire or exercise ability to imitate • Acquire or exercise notion of numbers and quantity
	Sensory stimulation	
	Space-time perception	
	Corporal awareness	
Cognitive Area	Atention and concentration	
	Recognition of categories	
	Memory	
	Language and communication	
Social-emotional Area	Presentation	
	Activity	
	Leave-taking and relaxation	
	Board games	

The objective of this game is for the individual to interact with the dog in a relaxing environment. It can be used as a sort of reinforcement or reward for the RI upon completing a task.

Several things must be done to prepare for a walk with the dog: he is brushed and outfitted with his bib (or sweater), his collar must be put on and the leash attached to it.

Either the RI is asked to go collect these items from the place they are kept, or he asks the dog to fetch them.

The dog remains calm and quiet while being readied, and then goes out with the RI for a walk. The dog accompanies the individual in the "heel" position.

Variations:

– Work with keeping track of colors and discriminating between them. Various dogs will be used, each one representing a color, with like-colored accessories.

– Work with categorizing different materials and objects.

– Work with reading skills at the time of choosing which dog to walk and identifying the basket containing that particular animal's accessories.

– The RI receives a part of the CTAC leash each time he gives a correct answer or follows an instruction. When he successfully assembles the leash, he gets to take the dog for a walk.

COMMANDS FOR THE DOG	MATERIALS
• Stand	• Brushes
• Sit	• Sweater or coat for dog
• Down	• Different type collars
• Stay	• Different leashes
• Fetch	• CTAC leash
• Give	• Colored die
• Heel	• Die with photos/names

SENSORIAL STIMULATION

		Objectives
Psychomotor Area	Physical coordination	• Reduce stress
	Sensory stimulation	• Enhance affective bond between the individual and the dog
	Space-time perception	• Engage in regular physical activity
	Corporal awareness	• Exercise gross motor skills
Cognitive Area	Atention and concentration	• Exercise fine motor skills
	Recognition of categories	• Exercise balance
	Memory	• Develop capacity to proceed step-by-step
	Language and communication	• Encourage social relationships
Social-emotional Area	Presentation	• Enhance self-esteem
	Activity	• Enjoy free time
	Leave-taking and relaxation	
	Board games	

The objective of this activity is to stimulate the RI's auditory perception.

To begin, we associate the sounds made by different instruments (tambourine, bell and rattle) with different modes of locomotion: walk, run and stop.

Once the RI understands these associations, we instruct him to begin walking with the dog in front of the IP while at the same time paying attention to the sounds (provided by the IP) that tell him whether to run, walk or stop.

Variations:

– We can use a single instrument, but vary the locomotion's speed from slow to fast and fast to slow.

– The IP can previously associate a hoop of a certain color with a particular sound. Depending on the sound made by the IP, the RI selects the correct hoop and has the dog jump through it.

– At the session's outset, the IP associates an object or a number with a particular sound. Depending on the sound made by the IP, the RI picks up the correct object and uses it to interact with the dog, or he gets however many treats are indicated by the associated number.

COMMANDS FOR THE DOG   MATERIALS

• Heel   • Musical instruments
• Walk   • Different colored hoops
• Run
• Stop
• Jump

	Physical coordination	Objectives
Psychomotor Area	Sensory stimulation	• Auditory stimulation
	Space-time perception	• Encourage listening
	Corporal awareness	• Exercise gross motor skills
Cognitive Area	Atention and concentration	• Exercise auditory perception and rhythm
	Recognition of categories	• Develop or evaluate short-term memory
	Memory	• Visually recognize numbers
	Language and communication	• Experience the pleasure of movement
Social-emotional Area	Presentation	
	Activity	
	Leave-taking and relaxation	
	Board games	

CONES AND TEXTURES

The objective of this activity is to reduce sensibility to different textures.

We situate a certain number of cones or mushrooms around the room.

On each on the IP places a piece of material with a distinctive texture such as sandpaper, a jar of lotion, a ball of yarn, etc.

Under each cone is an object the RI can use to interact with the dog (a brush, a ball, a bowl of food...).

Now the RI, accompanied by the dog, walks among the cones. When they reach a cone, the dog stops and lies down to indicate that the RI must pick up the material there and handle it.

If he does so to the IP's satisfaction, he can lift up the cone and identify the object (with eyes open or closed). Then, after naming it, he uses it to interact with the dog.

Variations:

– With the dog lying calmly in the "down" position, the RI caresses different parts of his body to identify various textures.for example:

- The nose is moist and cold.
- The tummy is smooth and warm.
- The paw pads are hard and rough, etc.

COMMANDS FOR THE DOG	MATERIALS
• Sit	• Cones
• Down	• Materials with different textures
• Heel	• Objects for interacting with
• Stay	the dog

		Objectives
Psychomotor Area	Physical coordination	• Exercise fine motor skills
	Sensory stimulation	• Exercise hand-eye coordination
	Space-time perception	• Exercise tactile perception
	Corporal awareness	• Exercise sense of taste
Cognitive Area	Atention and concentration	• Exercise sense of smell • Recognize objects
	Recognition of categories	• Develop symbolic thinking
	Memory	• Enrich vocabulary • Enhance tactile recognition
	Language and communication	• Experience the pleasure of using a tool
Social-emotional Area	Presentation	
	Activity	
	Leave-taking and relaxation	
	Board games	

THE PATH FOR GETTING DRESSED

The objective of this activity is for the RI to retain certain information and use it in dressing himself.

The RI and the dog make their way around a circuit formed by four cones. At the first cone, there are four different-colored balls, one of which the dog chooses. That becomes the key color; for example, red.

Then the RI and dog move on to the next cone, where they find four items of clothing. The RI must select the key-colored item, such as a pair of red socks.

Continuing on to the next cone, he finds four cards showing different parts of the body, and he must select the one illustrating that part where the item of clothing goes – in this case, the feet.

At the fourth and last cone, the dog sits beside the therapist and the RI. The RI must now select from an array of cards, or from a pocket on the dog's blanket, the card showing the item of clothing he has collected. In this case, he picks out the card showing a pair of red socks.

Lastly, he places the item of clothing on the IP or on himself.

Variations:

– Make the selections among items used in caring for or interacting with the dog.

– Use dog clothing.

COMMANDS FOR THE DOG	MATERIALS
• Fetch	• Cones
• Drop	• Items of clothing
• Stay	• Balls
• Get it	• Cards illustrating parts of body
	• CTAC dog blanket

		Objectives
Psychomotor Area	Physical coordination	• Exercise hand-eye coordination
	Sensory stimulation	• Exercise tactile perception
	Space-time perception	• Develop mental image of body
	Corporal awareness	• Acquire or exercise notion of color and sizes
Cognitive Area	Atention and concentration	• Synthesize the parts of a whole
	Recognition of categories	• Develop or evaluate short-term memory
	Memory	• Recognize the parts of a whole
	Language and communication	• Learn to listen and respond
		• Enrich vocabulary
Social-emotional Area	Presentation	• Establish relationships between objects
	Activity	
	Leave-taking and relaxation	
	Board games	

TOY TEXTURES

The objective of this activity is for the RI to play with the dog while using tactile perceptions.

To begin, the IP exhibits a ball with certain physical characteristics: size, weight, roughness of surface, pliability, vibrating or not, etc. The RI, with eyes open or shut, must register and memorize the ball's characteristics.

The dog then takes to the RI a bag containing his (the dog's) favorite balls.

The RI puts his hand in the bag and tries to find, by way of touch, a ball just like the one the IP exhibited at the beginning of the session.

If he picks the right one, he can throw it for the dog to fetch.

Variations:

– We place the dog lying down beside the RI, who, with his eyes closed, must identify the various parts of the dog's body by touch.

– Identify, by way of touch, the coat type of the different therapy dogs.

– The RI walks barefoot with the dog over surfaces of differing texture, varying his speed. Depending on the degree of trust the RI has in the dog, it can be the animal who sets the pace.

COMMANDS FOR THE DOG	MATERIALS
• Fetch • Drop • Give • Stand • Stay • Carry 	• Pairs of balls or toys of various textures and sizes • Basket • Blindfold

Psychomotor Area	Physical coordination	Objectives
	Sensory stimulation	• Exercise tactile perception
	Space-time perception	• Acquire or exercise ability to concentrate
	Corporal awareness	• Acquire or exercise notion of size
Cognitive Area	Atention and concentration	• Acquire or exercise notion of geometric shapes
	Recognition of categories	• Recognize objects
	Memory	• Experience the pleasure or achievement
	Language and communication	
Social-emotional Area	Presentation	
	Activity	
	Leave-taking and relaxation	
	Board games	

The objective of the game is for the RI to correctly identify colors.

We have five buttons in four different colors representing "super fleas." All the buttons are hidden on different parts of the body of one of the therapy dogs. The IP also has five clothespins, which represent an application of preventive medicine against ticks and fleas.

The objective is for the RI to place all the colored buttons in their like-colored baskets before the IP can attach the five clothespins to the dog.

The RI tosses a die whose facets show four different colors, in addition to a joker and a symbol for the anti-parasite medicine. Depending on the color that comes up, the RI must approach the "flea-bitten" dog and find the "super flea" of that same color. With the flea in hand – before putting it in its corresponding basket – the individual must perform a pre-established action.

For example, if the flea's color is blue, he must name something he likes; if it's red, he says something he dislikes; for green, he names one of his own qualities; for yellow, he names a quality of a companion.

If the toss of the die turns up the anti-flea and tick symbol, the technician places a clothespin on the dog. If the joker comes up, the IP or the RI can choose what color flea to take off the dog.

If the RI is able to put all the fleas in their right basket before the IP has attached all the clothespins, he wins the game.

Variations:

– Different areas of socialization can be incorporated.

COMMANDS FOR THE DOG	MATERIALS
• Down • Stay	• Colored buttons • Colors die • Clothespins

SENSORIAL STIMULATION

	Physical coordination	Objectives
Psychomotor Area	Sensory stimulation	• Exercise vision-body coordination • Exercise fine motor skills • Acquire or exercise ability to concentrate • Improve oral comprehension • Enrich vocabulary • Stimulate communication and group interaction • Learn and respect social norms • Learn to listen and respond • Experience the pleasure of guessing right • Experience the pleasure of achievement
	Space-time perception	
	Corporal awareness	
Cognitive Area	Atention and concentration	
	Recognition of categories	
	Memory	
	Language and communication	
Social-emotional Area	Presentation	
	Activity	
	Leave-taking and relaxation	
	Board games	

The objective of this exercise is to stimulate visual contact in order to improve communication.

At the outset, we emphasize the importance of visual contact between the RI and the dog, describing how it helps the animal understand what is being asked of him.

The technician puts on a brief demonstration. He gives the dog a command as he looks away from the animal which does not obey. But, when the command is repeated with good visual contact between the two, the dog obeys immediately.

The RIs take their place in the dog's line of sight and every time the dog looks squarely at one of them, he clicks his clicker. Then he gives a treat to the dog.

The IP asks the RI if he liked the feeling of being looked at by the dog squarely in the eyes, and what he felt.

Then the RI and the technician (or two RIs) sit down facing each other with the dog between them. They pet and caress the dog as a way of promoting the next visual contact.

Each time a RI looks at his co-RT or the AIT, the IP clicks his clicker. One of the RIs must now describe, while looking at his companion in the eyes, a trick or action he wants him to perform with the dog.

COMMANDS FOR THE DOG	MATERIALS
• Stay	• Clickers
• Treat	• Instructions
• Look	• CTAC dog blanket
• Stand	
• Get it	
• Various tricks and skills	

	Physical coordination	Objectives
Psychomotor Area	Sensory stimulation	• Reduce shyness and reticence
	Space-time perception	• Practice self-control
	Corporal awareness	• Practice social skills
Cognitive Area	Atention and concentration	• Develop the capacity to share in others' emotions
	Recognition of categories	• Develop the capacity to understand others
	Memory	• Increase tolerance of frustration
	Language and communication	• Create affective ties
Social-emotional Area	Presentation	• Increase personal and social well-being
	Activity	
	Leave-taking and relaxation	
	Board games	

CLICKING

The objective of this activity is to introduce the concept of fun and the working of the clicker.

After putting on a brief demonstration of the dog's tricks and skills, the AIT asks the RIs how they think the dog learned from them. One of the many responses will be that it was done with the help of this little instrument: the clicker.

At first we explain to the RIs how we "load" the clicker with regard to the dog. To do this, we use the clicker. We make a deal with the dog, telling him: "Every time you hear a 'click,' I'll give you a treat."

After several repetitions of the click-treat sequence, when the RI considers that the dog has understood this instruction, he takes a step forward and tells the dog: "Every time you do something well, you'll hear a click and you'll get a treat. On the other hand, if you do something poorly, I will ignore you and you won't get anything."

This is a good time to ask the RI what he likes to be told or what he likes to get when he does something well, and what he should be told if he does something poorly.

Now, with the theoretical part explained, we move on to the practical portion. The RI stands in front of the dog with the clicker in one hand and a treat in the other. When he makes visual contact with the dog, he activates the clicker and gives the dog a treat. If it is difficult to work with both hands, the AIT can perform some of the actions for him.

Each time the RI gives a treat to the dog, the AIT or the IP congratulates the RI for the good work he's doing. If there is more than one RI, the one standing in front of the dog can ask one of his companions to activate the clicker at the appropriate time. With two people, one clicks and the other gives the treat. At the end of the exercise, they congratulate each other for a job well done.

COMMANDS FOR THE DOG	MATERIALS
• Treat	• Clicker
• Stay	
• Look	

	Physical coordination	Objectives
Psychomotor Area	Sensory stimulation	• Exercise fine motor skills
	Space-time perception	• Exercise vision-body coordination
	Corporal awareness	• Exercise visual contact
Cognitive Area	Atention and concentration	• Exercise paying attention and concentration
	Recognition of categories	• Create affective ties
	Memory	• Codification and de-codification of symbols
	Language and communication	• Improve accuracy
Social-emotional Area	Presentation	• Set achievable goals
	Activity	
	Leave-taking and relaxation	
	Board games	

The objective of this activity is for the RI to interact in a relaxed way with the dog using his sense of touch.

We start with the RI naming the distinct textures on the dog's different body parts, such as:

Snout; moist and smooth
Ears; soft and silky
Paw pads; hard and rough
Nails; hard and sharp
Belly; smooth and warm
Tongue; moist and rough
Fangs; hard and smooth
Lips; moist and meaty

We place the dog on a table and cover the RI's eyes with a blindfold. He then walks around the table until he hears a clap or a previously agreed upon sound. He immediately places his hands on the dog and feels around that spot in order to identify the body part he's touching.

Variations:

– Identify the dog: We start by introducing each one of the AIT's dogs by name and pointing out his or her most noteworthy characteristics. Then we put them up on a big table and place a blindfold on an RI, who walks around the table until he hears a certain sound. He immediately puts his hands on the nearest dog and tries to guess which one it is (he may need some tips or hints). At the end of the game, the AIT gives each RI a treat to give to a dog.

– Identify the dog's body parts.

– We blindfold one RI and another select a dog and holds him. The first must find the dog by using his sense of touch and then identify the companion holding him.

COMMANDS FOR THE DOG	MATERIALS
• Down	• Large table
• Stay	• Blindfold
• Get it	

	Physical coordination	Objectives
Psychomotor Area	Sensory stimulation	• Exercise auditory perception
	Space-time perception	• Exercise tactile perception • Develop mental image of body
	Corporal awareness	structure
Cognitive Area	Atention and concentration	• Perception of tactile indicators • Acquire or exercise the notion of size
	Recognition of categories	• Establish relationships
	Memory	• Stimulate group communication and interaction
	Language and communication	• Learn and respect social norms • Improve memory
Social-emotional Area	Presentation	• Experience feeling of lack of sight • Promote good group dynamic
	Activity	
	Leave-taking and relaxation	
	Board games	

The objective of this activity is for the RI to get to know and perceive the dog through the sense of sight.

To start, the IP talks about the parts of the body involved in the sense of sight and the use we make of vision in our daily lives.

We can enrich the session by talking about blind or sight-impaired people and how the service dogs improve their quality of life – seeing-eye, or guide dogs.

Exercise 1:

We ask the RI to closely observe the dog and then describe or point out on a chart the skill the animal has just performed.

Variations:

– We show the RI a photo or illustration of a canine skill, then ask him to clap, click or cheer when the dog performs that skill.

Exercise 2:

If there is more than one therapy dog on hand, we ask the RI to observe them closely in order to find and describe the differences between them.

Exercise 3:

The AIT walks the dog around a course and the RI watches how he does it in order to repeat the walk.

Exercise 4:

Dress up a dog. The RI, after observing closely, dresses another dog in the same fashion. If there is only one dog, the RI can copy the dog's outfit from a photograph.

COMMANDS FOR THE DOG	MATERIALS
• Various skills and tricks • Stay • Heel • Forward (guide dog)	• Cards or chart of skills • Items for dressing dog

SIT	DOWN	SHAME
UP	COME	PUM
PAW	TWIST	CROQUETTE

		Objectives
Psychomotor Area	Physical coordination	• Exercise sight-space perception • Exercise visual perception: back ground-shape • Acquire or exercise ability to concentrate • Develop or evaluate visual memory • Develop capacity for observation • Exercise sight-body coordination • Experience sensation of lacking sight • Gain awareness of one's own capabilities and limitations
	Sensory stimulation	
	Space-time perception	
	Corporal awareness	
Cognitive Area	Atention and concentration	
	Recognition of categories	
	Memory	
	Language and communication	
Social-emotional Area	Presentation	
	Activity	
	Leave-taking and relaxation	
	Board games	

The objective is for the RI to perceive and describe the dog using the sense of touch.

The IP begins by talking about the sense of touch and the parts of the body we use to perceive different textures. Before beginning the exercise, the AIT must have in mind a mental list of how different parts of his dog's body feel to the touch: the nose, moist and viscous; the snout, soft and pointy; the ears, warm and fluffy; the paw pads, rough, spongy, creased, warm, etc.

We place the dog lying down on a table and have the RI toss the die showing the parts of the human body. If there are two dogs, the other retrieves the die and gives it to the RI, who identifies the part of his body he must now use to touch the dog: hand, arm, lips, forehead, nose, etc.

We can use different means of selecting the part of the dog's body to be touched: raise a cup hiding an image or a word, use a roulette wheel, pick a card from a fanned array, the dog carries the RI a card in his mouth or in his CTAC BestVest, etc.

We then ask the RI to touch that part of the dog's body and describe the sensations he feels. If that is not possible, we ask him to listen attentively to the IP's comments.

Variations:

– Present the RI with dog care or cleaning products such as shampoo or foam for him to use on the animal in order to experience new tactile sensations.

COMMANDS FOR THE DOG	MATERIALS
• Down and stay • Relax	• CTAC body parts die • Roulette wheel with parts of body • Dog care products: foam, gel, etc.

		Objectives
Psychomotor Area	Physical coordination	• Exercise tactile perception • Develop mental image of body structure • Mitigate tactile hyper-sensitivity • Develop and control muscular strength • Perceive tactile indicators • Improve tactile recognition • Experience the pleasure of getting messy • Experience the pleasure of guessing right • Practice self-control
	Sensory stimulation	
	Space-time perception	
	Corporal awareness	
Cognitive Area	Atention and concentration	
	Recognition of categories	
	Memory	
	Language and communication	
Social-emotional Area	Presentation	
	Activity	
	Leave-taking and relaxation	
	Board games	

The objective of this activity is for the RI to get to know and perceive the dog by way of the sense of hearing. To start off, the IP talks about the parts of the human body involved in auditory perception, and about how we use the sense of hearing in our daily lives. Here we can expand the discussion to include mention of people with hearing impairments and specially trained "signal" dogs that help those individuals in their day-to-day activities.

Exercise 1:

Count the dog's barks.

Exercise 2:

Identify different emotional states of dogs by using audiotapes of the sounds they make, along with photographs or illustrations.

Exercise 3:

Listen closely to the internal sounds the dog makes by having the RI press his ear lightly on the prostrate animal's thorax or belly in order to listen to the heartbeat and breathing, the peristaltic (intestinal) movement and assorted wheezes or puffs.

Exercise 4:

We show the RI a series of opaque closed jars. Each one contains a different material that, upon being shaken, makes a particular sound. The IP mentions that one of the jars holds something the dog likes a great deal: treats. If the RI can guess which jar that is, he gets to give the dog the treats. After shaking and listening to each one, and guessing as to what is inside, the RI tells the dog to put his paw on a certain one. If it is the one with the treats, the RI gives the dog one or more in exchange for performing a trick or skill.

Variations:

We have three opaque jars; under one of them we hide a treat. The IP moves the three jars (as in a shell game) under the attentive eye of the RI. When he stops, the dog must guess which jar covers the treat. The RI jiggles that jar in order to hear if it makes a noise.

COMMANDS FOR THE DOG	MATERIALS
• Down	• Jars with beans, rice, coins
• Stay	• Treats
• Speak	• Cards

SENSORIAL STIMULATION

		Objectives
Psychomotor Area	Physical coordination	• Exercise sense of rhythm • Exercise auditory perception and discrimination • Control breathing • Stimulate auditory perception
	Sensory stimulation	
	Space-time perception	
	Corporal awareness	
Cognitive Area	Atention and concentration	
	Recognition of categories	
	Memory	
	Language and communication	
Social-emotional Area	Presentation	
	Activity	
	Leave-taking and relaxation	
	Board games	

The objective is for the RI to perceive and describe the dog by using his sense of smell. The IP starts the session off by talking about the sense of smell, what parts of the body are involved in it and how we use it in our daily lives.

Before beginning, the AIT must keep in mind the way different parts of his dog's body smell in order to help the RI describe those smells.

Exercise 1:

We ask the RI to smell different parts of the dog's body. In choosing which part to begin with, we keep in mind the particular characteristics of the RI and how we want to work with him on fine motor skills, psycho-motor activity, memory, willingness, etc. For exemple, we can explore the inside of the ear, the mouth, the shoulders, paw pads, trunk, tail, etc.

Exercise 2:

The IP hides a treat in one hand. The RI then smells both of the IP's hands to determine which holds the treat. He then has the dog perform the same action to corroborate his choice. If the RI and the dog pick the same hand, the IP opens it. If the treat is there, the RI gives it to the dog in exchange for a trick. If it's the wrong hand, the dog "commands" the RI to do a little trick.

Exercise 3:

It's important for the RI to learn and acknowledge his own capabilities and limitations, a process that will help him appreciate the abilities of others (including the dog's).

We ask him to close his eyes and use only his sense of smell to find a hidden treat. Since this will be difficult, he can ask for verbal clues until he locates it. Then the RI hides a treat or an object, and tells the dog, whose sense of smell is superior, to find it.

COMMANDS FOR THE DOG	MATERIALS
• Sit • Mark	• Roulette wheel of parts of body • CTAC die or BestVest dog blanket

		Objectives
Psychomotor Area	Physical coordination	• Exercise sense of smell
	Sensory stimulation	• Exercise olfactory perception and discrimination
	Space-time perception	• Acquire or exercise ability to concentrate
	Corporal awareness	• Develop or evaluate olfactory memory
Cognitive Area	Atention and concentration	• Enrich vocabulary
	Recognition of categories	• Promote self-awareness
	Memory	• Learn and acknowledge capabilities and limitations
	Language and communication	
Social-emotional Area	Presentation	
	Activity	
	Leave-taking and relaxation	
	Board games	

The objective of this exercise is for the RI to be able to identify the basic elements of taste and distinguish between sweet, salty, tart and bitter. We will proceed by gradually increasing the activity's complexity, beginning with flavors the RI likes the best before adding other flavors to those being tasted.

The RI is seated next to the EAI with the dog in front of them. The dog, according to commands from the TAI, will go to the jar containing the particular food or substance the EAI wants the give to the RI to try. Every time the RI tastes a new flavor, the dog will perform a skill or trick.

Let's use an example. Suppose we are working with something sweet, such as honey. When the EAI takes a spoonful from the jar (which can be identified with a specific color, or not) for the RI to taste, the dog will perform a Twist while the EAI says the word "sweet."

The process is repeated with different sweet foods or candies and, each time the RI tastes something sweet, he says the word "sweet," which prompts the dog to perform the skill or trick associated with that flavor. When the RI is consistently able to identify that flavor, we proceed to a new one, associated with a different trick.

The game becomes more complex when the RI, with his eyes closed, must say the names of the flavors out loud as they are picked at random. If the answer is correct, he opens his eyes to see the dog perform the specific trick. If the answer is incorrect, the RI is aided visually by seeing the dog sitting beside the jar (colored or not, as desired) containing items of the flavor being tasted.

When the RI is able to consistently identify two (or three) flavors, we introduce a third (or fourth) and proceed to work with all three (or four) at once.

COMMANDS FOR THE DOG	MATERIALS
· Sit	· 4 jars, either colored or
· Stand	without identification
· Get it	· Foodstuffs of various flavors
· Various tricks and skills	· Blindfold
	· Spoons

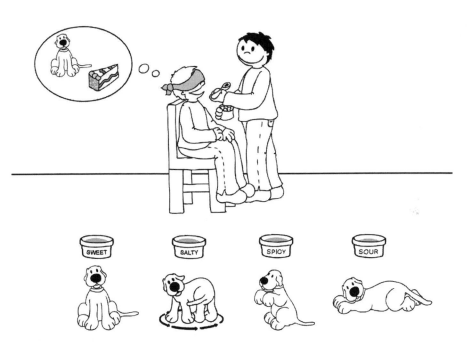

	Physical coordination	Objectives
Psychomotor Area	Sensory stimulation	· Exercise sight-space perception
	Space-time perception	· Exercise sense of left-right · Exercise sense of balance
	Corporal awareness	· Acquire or exercise the notion of symmetry
Cognitive Area	Atention and concentration	· Imitate movements: body control
	Recognition of categories	· Pay attention to movements of others
	Memory	· Acquire or exercise the ability to imitate
	Language and communication	· Express feelings: sadness, happiness, anger
Social-emotional Area	Presentation	· Experience the pleasure of control of an object
	Activity	
	Leave-taking and relaxation	
	Board games	

We can use the affective bond between the RI and the dog to help the RI incorporate new foods into his diet. We can do this by using the food we want to work with – probably a fruit or vegetable – in much the same way we use the dog treats, which at a certain point are withdrawn from this exercise.

At first we work with objects. The RI hands over different objects, such as hoops, cones, mushrooms, etc, to members of the therapy team.

Then we move on to dog treats. The IP gives a treat to the RI, who either gives it directly to the dog or hands it to another member of the group to give to the dog.

In the third stage we introduce the new food. The IP gives this food to the RI with the instruction that he either eat it, or give it to another member of the team. If the RI decides to try to eat it and puts it in his mouth, the process of chewing and swallowing it can be facilitated by giving the RI another dog treat to give to the dog while he chews and swallows. Over time, the interval between swallowing the new food and giving the dog a treat will be lengthened. Once the RI tolerates and ingests the new food, he can have some more of it during a period of re-affirmation.

In concluding this activity, we bring back into play the dog treats for the RI to give the animal at the appropriate time (such as after performing a trick), while the RI eats the new food as a separate activity.

COMMANDS FOR THE DOG

- Sit
- Treat
- Get it
- Give
- Carry

MATERIALS

- Foods to incorporate in diet
- Distracting elements: kerchiefs, hoops, balls...

		Objectives
Psychomotor Area	Physical coordination	• Exercise sense of taste
	Sensory stimulation	• Exercise sense of smell
	Space-time perception	• Exercise sense of touch
	Corporal awareness	• Pay attention to instructions
Cognitive Area	Atention and concentration	• Learn participants' names
	Recognition of categories	• Improve oral comprehension
	Memory	
	Language and communication	
Social-emotional Area	Presentation	
	Activity	
	Leave-taking and relaxation	
	Board games	

The objective of this activity is to reinforce the RI's visual contact.

The activity's difficulty can be increased according to the degree of attention and concentration exhibited by the RI.

The RI and the IP sit across from each other at a small table. Every time the RI looks at the treat on the table, he can give it to the dog, who will perform a trick or skill in return.

Then we cover the treat with a transparent plastic glass that the IP moves around the table while the RI observes the movement. If he follows the movement, the RI can then lift the glass, pick up the treat and give it to the dog.

The length of time the glass is moved around the table is gradually increased. We can increase the difficulty by using two or three transparent glasses in movement, but only one containing a treat. In a later stage, we can use opaque glasses.

The dog can be used to help guess the location of the treat by touching a certain glass with his paw.

Variations:

– We can stimulate further communication by asking the RI to say "Treat!" before raising the glass and then have him, with the help of the technician if needed, command the dog to perform a trick or skill.

– Observe the dog's movements around the room, then repeat them alongside the animal.

COMMANDS FOR THE DOG	MATERIALS
• Sit	• Table
• Treat	• Chairs
• Mark	• Transparent glasses
• Various skills and tricks	• Opaque glasses
	• Skills cards or chart

	Physical coordination	Objectives
Psychomotor Area	Sensory stimulation	• Attention and concentration
	Space-time perception	• Visual following of an object
	Corporal awareness	• Develop motor skills: pick up, let go, raise
Cognitive Area	Atention and concentration	• Exercise visual perception: back ground-shape
	Recognition of categories	• Pay attention to movement
	Memory	• Acquire or exercise ability to concentrate
	Language and communication	• Develop or evaluate visual memory
Social-emotional Area	Presentation	• Develop or evaluate visual-space perception
	Activity	• Exercise sight-body coordination
	Leave-taking and relaxation	• Experience the pleasure of achievement
	Board games	

The objective of this activity is for the RI to enjoy thinking about and making a surprise gift for the dog.

We can adjust the project's degree of complexity.

- We can suggest specific objects to make, provide the necessary materials and guide him in the construction.
- We present him with an array of materials, invite him to use them to create something and help with the work.
- He comes up with the idea for an object, finds the materials and builds it on his own.

We can make different gifts and wrap them:

- A ball of wool: a wool pom-pom
- A Styrofoam ball decorated with construction paper, pieces of fabric...
- A ball made of a balloon with water: We fill a balloon partially with water (not to the point of bursting), tie a knot and cut off the excess "tail." Other balloons can then be attached to the ball. This can also be done using rice instead of water.
- A decorated shoe on a clay stand
- A chew toy made of knotted socks
- A rattle made from a decorated plastic container
- A decorated bowl, leash or collar
- A bone decorated with wishes
- A decorated frame for photographs

The dog helps the RI in any way he can (bringing him materials, pulling on the wool in making a pom-pom, barking to show approval, etc.) or simply sits and watches attentively while the RI works. When the gift is presented, the dog shows his gratitude and uses the gift.

COMMANDS FOR THE DOG	MATERIALS
• Tug	• Socks
• Sit and stay	• Large bottles of water
• Fetch and give	• Wool
• Look	• Colored tape and adhesives, fabrics, stones
• Speak	• Balloons
• Kiss	• Rice
✍	• Water

		Objectives
Psychomotor Area	Physical coordination	• Create an affective bond
	Sensory stimulation	• Exercise sight-body coordination
	Space-time perception	• Express fantasies
	Corporal awareness	• Learn to plan
Cognitive Area	Atention and concentration	• Learn to solve problems
	Recognition of categories	• Learn to express interest in others
	Memory	• Develop capacity to enjoy positive feelings
	Language and communication	• Experience the pleasure of imposing one's will on an object
Social-emotional Area	Presentation	
	Activity	
	Leave-taking and relaxation	
	Board games	

The objective of this activity is to spark interest in the dog among those RIs with attention deficit or visual impairment. We help them perceive the dog's movements by way of touch and sounds.

The RI will be in near-constant physical contact with the dog, with his hands touching various parts of the animal's body while the dog is in different positions. The AIT will be placing different sound-making devices on the dog to provide additional input to the RI regarding the animal's movements.

"Sit": The AIT places on the dog's withers a cylindrical rattle so that when he sits the rattle rolls off his back and falls noisily to the floor. The RI places his hand on the dog's croup and pronounces the command, "Sit."

"Paw": The AIT places a rattle bracelet on each of the dog's front feet. The RI holds out his hand palm up. When the says, "Paw," the dog places a foot on the outstretched hand, making a noise with his bracelet.

"Come" and "Stop": The AIT puts rattle bracelets on each of the dog's four feet so that, when moving toward the RI the animal makes noise and upon stopping the noise ceases. The RI makes a "come here" motion with his hands and arms to get the dog to move toward him and while he hears the sound of the rattles. When the dog reaches him and stops, the RI extends his arms, palms out.

"Belly": With the dog lying down face up, we help the RI stroke the animal's belly.

COMMANDS FOR THE DOG	MATERIALS
• Sit	• Sound-making objects
• Stay	• Rattles
• Come	• Shakers
• Paw	• Tambourine
• Belly	• Piano

	Physical coordination	Objectives
Psychomotor Area	Sensory stimulation	• Exercise gross motor skills
	Space-time perception	• Exercise auditory perception
	Corporal awareness	• Develop mental image of body structure
Cognitive Area	Atention and concentration	• Pay attention to instructions
	Recognition of categories	• Pay attention to movement of others
	Memory	• Improve recognition by touch
	Language and communication	• Promote bond forming
Social-emotional Area	Presentation	
	Activity	
	Leave-taking and relaxation	
	Board games	

The objective is to help the RI tolerate and eventually enjoy having sunscreen or moisturizing cream applied to his skin.

If applying cream or sunscreen is a problem, this exercise will help him realize that the application leads to doing pleasurable things such as going to the park to play on the slide with the dog or going to the beach with his family.

We have seen that taking advantage of the bond between the RI and the dog helps make this exercise very effective.

When we do our daily grooming of the dog, while we brush and pet him or her, we point out to the RI that the paw pads are dry and cracked. We lift the foot and have him stroke the pads from the bent joint outwards to feel how rough they are. Then we invite him to help take care of the pads.

We do this in small steps, consolidating each bit of progress so we won't have to go back and start again from the beginning.

1. To start, the AIT puts some cream on the paw pad, begins rubbing it in and asks the RI to help him spread it.

2. The AIT puts some cream in his own palm, and both he and the RI take dabs from there to spread on the paw pad.

3. The IP puts cream on the palm of the RI, and they both then apply it to the pad.

4. The IP puts cream on the palm of the RI, who then must rub his two hands together before applying it to the paw pads.

5. The RI takes the container of cream, scoops or squeezes some on to his own palm, rubs his hands together and applies the cream to the dog's paws.

COMMANDS FOR THE DOG	MATERIALS
• Down	• Grooming kit
• Stay	• Brush
	• Paper towels
	• Moisturizing cream

SENSORIAL STIMULATION

	Physical coordination	Objectives
Psychomotor Area	Sensory stimulation	• Exercise gross motor skills
	Space-time perception	• Exercise fine motor skills
	Corporal awareness	• Exercise tactile perception • Exercise olfactory perception
Cognitive Area	Atention and concentration	• Develop idea of body structure • Learn and respect social norms
	Recognition of categories	• Experience the pleasure of
	Memory	achievement
	Language and communication	• Mitigate hyper-sensitivity
Social-emotional Area	Presentation	
	Activity	
	Leave-taking and relaxation	
	Board games	

The objective of this activity is to use contact with the dog to provide basic sensory stimulation to persons affected to a greater degree by behavior disorders, with or without voluntary collaborative movement and productive language use.

In order for this to be effective, the surroundings must be tranquil and comfortable and we must make sure all our movements and those of the dog are gentle and calm and that our tone of voice is pleasant and harmonious.

We will be working with a therapy dog that has special characteristics, one we've dubbed a BLANKET DOG. What makes him or her particularly suited for this type of therapeutic exercise is an especially calm and steady personality, a strong sense of obedience, enhanced ability to handle being touched and manipulated and a high-degree of self-control so as to be able to remain relaxed throughout the activity in the various positions ordered by the AIT. These special characteristics are what will maximize interaction with the RI by way of multiple sensory channels.

We take into account that, in most cases, the RI will be seated, with little voluntary movement and perhaps a degree of physical frailty or reluctance. We must utilize different postures of the dog to maximize interaction between the person and the animal, always taking care that excessive weight not be placed on the RI. Stools and auxiliary tables can be used to make sure that does not happen.

The activities' objectives are pursued by placing the dog on a table or stool in a way that promotes physical contact between the RI and the dog: the RI petting the dog, the dog caressing or nuzzling the RI, controlled touching by the dog of a part of the RI's body, and guided giving of treats to the dog.

COMMANDS FOR THE DOG	MATERIALS
• Steady	• Stools
• Down	• Auxiliary tables
• Treat	• Skin cream for massages
• Stay	

SENSORIAL STIMULATION

		Objectives
Psychomotor Area	Physical coordination	• Enhance sense of calmness and safety
	Sensory stimulation	
	Space-time perception	• Diminish physical nervousness
	Corporal awareness	• Establish verbal or gesture-based communication between the RI and the IP and/or the AIT
Cognitive Area	Atention and concentration	
	Recognition of categories	• Establish verbal or gesture-based communication. between the RI and the dog
	Memory	
	Language and communication	• Maximize comfort level
Social-emotional Area	Presentation	• Improve use of memory by recalling previous experience with pets that the RI may have had
	Activity	
	Leave-taking and relaxation	
	Board games	

cognitive stimulation exercises

cognitive

stimulation

exercises

DOG BINGO

The objective of this game is for the RI to pay close attention to the movements and postures of the dog and match them with their illustration on a card like those used in bingo games.

Each RI gets a card with a grid whose boxes contain illustrations of dog tricks or postures: sit, down, spinning circles, etc. We can increase complexity by including the direction involved in a specific trick, such as spinning to the right or to the left.

The dog effects a series of tricks or responses to commands, and the RIs mark the appropriate box on their cards with a dogbone or a treat.

When one of the players completes a line, he says "Bow." When he fills the entire card, he shouts out the name of the dog.

Variations:

- The boxes on the cards can show dogs with different colored and different sized hoops on various parts of their body.

- The dog gets the bingo card, instead of the RI. The RI then helps the dog as the game proceeds. Taking turns, the RIs select from a basket a card on which is written a mathematical operation. When the answer is determined, the dog marks the box numbered with the result. When a line is completed, the dog does a trick, and when the entire card is filled, he performs a previously established action or task.

COMMANDS FOR THE DOG	MATERIALS
• Tricks	• Skills cards
• Stay	• Hoops cards
• Fetch	• Chips
• Drop	• Math problem cards
• Get it	• Number cards

		Objectives
Psychomotor Area	Physical coordination	• Pay attention to other's movements
	Sensory stimulation	• Acquire notion of numbers and quantity
	Space-time perception	• Acquire notion of colors
	Corporal awareness	• Acquire notion of sizes
Cognitive Area	Atention and concentration	• Visually recognize numbers
	Recognition of categories	• Develop logical-mathematical thinking
	Memory	• Acquire notions of arithmetic; addition, subtraction
	Language and communication	• Learn and respect norms of social behavior
Social-emotional Area	Presentation	• Experience the pleasure of achievement
	Activity	
	Leave-taking and relaxation	
	Board games	

The objective of the game is for the RI to identify the differences between two dogs.

We place two dogs of different breeds in the same position in front of the RI. The individual, with the help of the IP, looks for physical differences between the two animals such as: the tail, the ears, height, coat color and length, snout, etc.

We can also put the dogs in different postures, or use props such as a table, chairs or boxes. The RI can then observe and describe differences between the positions of certain body parts of the two dogs.

Variations:

– Using two dogs, we decorate one with seven different colored handkerchiefs on various parts of his body. We then ask the RI to place seven identical handkerchiefs on the other dog without using one of the same color in the same place it appears on the first dog. We draw on paper a dog in the same position and context as the two therapy dogs.

– The RI, without speaking, makes marks on the drawing where he observes differences between the two. Both dogs are wearing some colored handkerchiefs, without any color being repeated. The RI is asked to closely observe the animals and make a mental note of what colors each one is wearing.

– He then tosses the color die and must recall and say which of the two dogs is wearing the color that comes up. If he is correct, he gets to remove that color handkerchief.

COMMANDS FOR THE DOG	MATERIALS
• Stay	• Handkerchiefs
• Hide	• Boxes
• Sit	• Table
• Down	• Chair
• Stand	

COGNITIVE STIMULATION

		Objectives
Psychomotor Area	Physical coordination	• Exercise visual-space perception • Exercise sense of place in space • Identify objects • Recognize the presence or absence of objects or people • Detect the absence of a crucial detail • Develop observation skills • Enhance memory
	Sensory stimulation	
	Space-time perception	
	Corporal awareness	
Cognitive Area	Atention and concentration	
	Recognition of categories	
	Memory	
	Language and communication	
Social-emotional Area	Presentation	
	Activity	
	Leave-taking and relaxation	
	Board games	

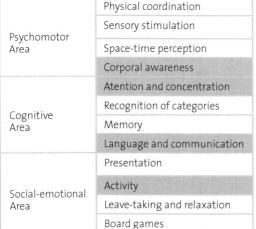

The objective of the game is for the RI to closely observe an action so as to be able to describe it and imitate it.

The IP and the dog together complete a relatively complex circuit along a course with obstacles such as chairs, benches, rollers, hurdles, etc.

The RI closely observes the circuit in order to be able to recreate it. Once he does that, he and the dog go along the course imitating the movements or tricks performed when the dog did it with the IP.

The IP will follow them at a certain distance to make sure the dog obeys the commands given by the RI.

If other individuals are taking part, the therapist can ask them to describe what they watched their companion do, and whether they noticed any mistakes.

Variations:

– The therapist asks the RI to closely observe the circuit he makes with the dog. If the description is accurate, the RI gets to do the course with the dog.

– If the RI has trouble communicating verbally, he can describe the circuit using hand signals or with the skills cards. If the description is accurate, he gets to do the course with the dog.

COMMANDS FOR THE DOG

• Heel
• General commands

MATERIALS

• Leash
• Skills cards
• Directional cards

	Physical coordination	Objectives
Psychomotor Area	Sensory stimulation	• Exercise gross motor skills
	Space-time perception	• Exercise visual-space perception
		• Exercise sense of place in space
	Corporal awareness	• Exercise orientation in time
Cognitive Area	Atention and concentration	• Pay attention to movement of others
	Recognition of categories	• Acquire or exercise ability to imitate
	Memory	• Enrich vocabulary
	Language and communication	• Enhance verbal expression
	Presentation	• Experience the pleasure of movement
Social-emotional Area	Activity	
	Leave-taking and relaxation	
	Board games	

COGNITIVE STIMULATION

135

The objective of this game is for the RI to pay close attention to a series of actions performed by the dog in order to be able to repeat them.

First we explain to the RI the different actions or tricks the dog is going to perform. We show him photographs of the tricks and we teach him to give the appropriate commands by both spoken word and gesture.

After the RI has practiced this, the IP will present him with a sequence of actions or tricks, either using photographs or by physical demonstration. Then the RI is asked to repeat the sequence. If he does this successfully, he gets to give the dog a treat.

This exercise can be simplified by associating each trick with a certain color.

The series or sequence can be laid out on the floor using colored moles to help the RI remember which trick is to be performed at each point on the circuit.

Variations:

- The RI can fashion a collar or a leash for the dog taking cues from a certain series of actions. He can then put them on the dog and take him for a walk.

- Others series can be effected by way of placing different shaped or different colored adhesive labels on the dog's back.

- Another series could be a sequence for gently touching the different parts of the dog's body

COMMANDS FOR THE DOG	MATERIALS
• Previously established tricks or skills	• Materials for making collars
• Stay	• Labels of differing color, shape and size
• Heel	• Colored hoops or mushrooms
	• Skills cards
	• Drawings of series of skills

COGNITIVE STIMULATION

		Objectives
Psychomotor Area	Physical coordination	• Develop concept of body structure
	Sensory stimulation	• Acquire or exercise ability to concentrate
	Space-time perception	• Acquire or exercise notion of numbers and quantity
	Corporal awareness	• Acquire or exercise sense of colors
Cognitive Area	Atention and concentration	• Acquire or exercise notion of sizes
	Recognition of categories	• Acquire or exercise notion of geometric shapes
	Memory	• Codification and de-codification of symbols
	Language and communication	• Accept rules for social interaction
Social-emotional Area	Presentation	• Experience the pleasure of achievement
	Activity	
	Leave-taking and relaxation	
	Board games	

The objective of this game is for the RI to find certain objects belonging to the dog that are "lost" in the room.

Before the session begins, the IP hides some items or the cards illustrating those items. He then assigns the RI a task.

The RI either spins the roulette wheel or tosses the color die to select a certain color. Then he and the dog begin their search for the objects they need in order to perform their task.

The can pick up only those items or cards of the color that came up and only those that will be of use in performing the task. When he finds an item fulfilling those two criteria, he takes it and, accompanied by the dog, uses it to carry out the task.

Variations:

– Packing a bag. The RI helps the dog pack a bag for a trip. The dog gives the RI a list of items needed for the trip, or they will draw up the list together. Starting with the first item, the two look for it among other objects in their field of vision. When they find the correct object, the dog places it in the bag.

– The shopping list. Before the less, we draw up a shopping list. After memorizing as many items as he can, the RI and the dog select from among arrayed items those that they recall from the list.

COMMANDS FOR THE DOG	MATERIALS
• Sit	• Objects cards
• Stay	• Items pertaining to the dog
• Fetch	• Toiletries for humans
• Carry	
• Mark	
• Heel	

$$\begin{array}{r} 3 \\ + 4 \\ \hline 7 \end{array}$$

COGNITIVE STIMULATION

		Objectives
Psychomotor Area	Physical coordination	
	Sensory stimulation	• Pay attention to instructions
	Space-time perception	• Acquire or exercise the ability to concentrate
	Corporal awareness	• Improve oral comprehension
Cognitive Area	Atention and concentration	• Develop or evaluate visual memory
	Recognition of categories	• Develop or evaluate short-term memory
	Memory	• Recognize objects
	Language and communication	• Recognize properties of objects
		• Develop symbolic thinking
Social-emotional Area	Presentation	• Enrich vocabulary
	Activity	• Stimulate active listening
	Leave-taking and relaxation	
	Board games	

139

The objective of this game is to form pairs consisting of a photograph of a particular dog skill and the written or hand-signal command to perform that skill.

The IP gives a hand-signal command to the dog, who obeys the command.

The RI pays close attention in order to be able to match the photo illustrating that skill with a card on which the command is written.

After the dog has obeyed a certain number of commands, the RI checks to see if the pairs have been made correctly. Taking each pair one-by-one, he reads the command out loud to see if the dog performs the skill illustrated in the photo making up the other half of the pair.

Variations:

– The RI tosses the skills die and then writes on a piece of paper the corresponding command. Then he gives that command orally to the dog to see if his identification was correct.

– The RI reads or listens to a story in which a dog performs various skills. He must identify them as he pronounces or hears them. Then, in a second reading or narration, he commands the dog to perform them at the points they come up in the story.

COMMANDS FOR THE DOG	MATERIALS
• Hand-signal commands	• Skills die
• Various skills or tricks	• Photographs of skills
• Stay	• Cards with written commands
	• Pencils
	• Paper
	• Treats

	Physical coordination	Objectives
Psychomotor Area	Sensory stimulation	• Pay attention to instructions • Pay attention to movements of others • Acquire or exercise the ability to concentrate • Improve oral comprehension • Acquire or exercise distinguishing between sounds • Develop language skills: expression and comprehension • Stimulate active listening • Experience the pleasure of achievement
	Space-time perception	
	Corporal awareness	
Cognitive Area	Atention and concentration	
	Recognition of categories	
	Memory	
	Language and communication	
Social-emotional Area	Presentation	
	Activity	
	Leave-taking and relaxation	
	Board games	

COGNITIVE STIMULATION

The objective of this game is for the RI to employ and improve his skills with numbers.

The RI tosses a numbered die to the dog, who returns it to him showing the number that came up. The RI commands the dog to perform a certain trick or skill that number of times.

As the dog obeys, the RI counts the repetitions out loud so that the dog knows when to stop. The RI then gives the dog that same number of treats.

The number can also be determined by an arithmetical operation. The resulting number will be the number of times the dog performs the trick or skill.

Variations:

– This exercise can be used to help the RI get used to being close to the dog. The RI tosses the numbered die to the dog, who picks it up and moves very slowly to the RI until he reaches him.

– The number that came up is the number of treats the RI gives to the dog, with the animal moving closer and closer with each successive toss.

– The IP places some treats in the RI's open hand. The RI, with his eyes closed, brings his hands together and, using his sense of touch, determines how many treats there are before giving them to the dog.

– After assigning each skill a number and memorizing them, the RI tosses the die and, depending on which number came up, gives the dog the corresponding command.

COMMANDS FOR THE DOG	MATERIALS
• Fetch • Drop • Stay • Treat 	• Classic or numbered die • Treats • Skills cards

	Physical coordination	Objectives
Psychomotor Area	Sensory stimulation	• Pay attention to movements of others
	Space-time perception	• Acquire or exercise ability to concentrate
	Corporal awareness	• Acquire or exercise notion of numbers and quantity
Cognitive Area	Atention and concentration	• Acquire or exercise arithmetical skills
	Recognition of categories	• Establish relationships between distinct elements
	Memory	
	Language and communication	
Social-emotional Area	Presentation	
	Activity	
	Leave-taking and relaxation	
	Board games	

COGNITIVE STIMULATION

The objective of this game is for the RI to put together a puzzle with the pieces he earns in each stage of the exercise.

We position mushrooms on the floor in a grid. Under each mushroom is a card illustrating a skill or an action.

The therapist tells the RI where to go, for example:
– Move two mushrooms forward
– Go back one mushroom
– Move two mushrooms to the right
– Go to the red mushroom

The RI lifts up the appropriate mushroom, examines the card and performs the skill or action indicated on it. If he does this correctly, he earns a puzzle piece, which the dog holds for him in a pouch on his coat.

After lifting all the mushrooms and earning all the pieces, the RI sits down with the dog and puts the puzzle together.

Variations:

– We can lay out a circuit with the mushrooms, each one of which hides a skills card, as a sort of obstacle course for the RI or for the dog.

– We can give the RI a "treasure map" to figure out in order to find, along with the dog, a reward.

COMMANDS FOR THE DOG	MATERIALS
• Tricks	• Mushrooms
• Sit	• Skills cards
	• Actions cards
	• Puzzle pieces
	• Treasure map
	• Treasure

COGNITIVE STIMULATION

		Objectives
Psychomotor Area	Physical coordination	• Acquire or exercise notion of direction • Exercise sense of place in space • Pay attention to instructions • Acquire or exercise notion of numbers and quantity • Acquire and exercise notion of colors • Make separate parts into a whole (puzzle) • Recognize objecgts • Develop symbolic thinking: codifying and de-codifying symbols • Cooperation: stimulate helpful relationships • Enhance self-esteem
	Sensory stimulation	
	Space-time perception	
	Corporal awareness	
Cognitive Area	Atention and concentration	
	Recognition of categories	
	Memory	
	Language and communication	
Social-emotional Area	Presentation	
	Activity	
	Leave-taking and relaxation	
	Board games	

CLASSIFYING THINGS

The objective of this game is to help the dog put things in order according to type.

The RI and IP are seated beside each other in front of a chest or a hoop containing different three-dimensional objects, or cards representing various objects. Later, the dog will be seated in front of a series of different colored boxes, one box for each of the "types" of objects in the chest.

The RI, with the IP's help, selects an object from the chest, describes it, and calls the dog to come take it and place it in its "right" box. The right box in which it should go into is determined by an attached card indicating its group or type.

Variations:

– With this same set-up, it is now the dog who starts things off. He chooses a box and stands or sits in front of it. The RI, with the IP's help, must no select from the chest an object of the type indicated by the color of the box chosen by the dog. He then takes this over to the box close to the dog. If the item belongs in that box, the dog picks it up and puts it in. If it does not, he barks or covers his eyes with a paw (the "Shame" command).

COMMANDS FOR THE DOG	MATERIALS
• Sit	• Objects to be classified
• Get it	• Different colored boxes
• Stay	• Cards indicating "type" of objects
• Come	
• Fetch	
• Drop	
• Shame	
• Speak	

COGNITIVE STIMULATION

	Physical coordination	Objectives
Psychomotor Area	Sensory stimulation	• Acquire or exercise ability to imitate
	Space-time perception	• Acquire or exercise ability to concentrate
	Corporal awareness	• Acquire or exercise ability to symbolize
Cognitive Area	Atention and concentration	• Recognize objects
	Recognition of categories	• Establish relationships between objects
	Memory	• Recognize properties of objects
	Language and communication	• Enrich vocabulary
Social-emotional Area	Presentation	• Improve pronunciation
	Activity	• Improve language comprehension and expression
	Leave-taking and relaxation	• Cooperation: Stimulate helpful relationships
	Board games	

The objective of this game is for the RI to tell the dog to do a trick according to what comes up on a toss of the colors die.

We show the RI various photographs of tricks the dog can do and he must describe them, understand them and imitate them, with or without the aid of the IP. We instruct him how to correctly deliver each command.

He then places each of the cards on a different colored plate. At first, the cards are face up, so he can associate each trick or skill with a color. Then the cards are turned face down, obliging the RI to memorize the relationships.

The RI tosses the color die and the dog either fetches it or the RI sees from his position which color has come up.

The RI gives the dog the command he associates with that color. When the dog has obeyed the command, the card on that color plate is turned over to show whether the RI remembered correctly.

When all the tricks have been performed the number of times deemed appropriate, we can continue exercising memory skills by completing sequences with the help of the dog. The dog brings each plate one-by-one, indicating in this way the order in which he wants the RI to give him the commands.

Variations:

– Once each skill or trick has been described, a companion is asked to observe closely and activate a clicker or clap his hands precisely when an action has been successfully completed, so the dog knows he has performed correctly.

– Shapes, sizes or everyday objects can be used instead of color as the indicator.

COMMANDS FOR THE DOG	MATERIALS
• Various skills or tricks	• Skills cards
• Hand-gesture and verbal commands	• Indicator objects: colored plates
• No	geometric shapes
• Get it	everyday items
• Cobrar	• Clicker
• Drop	• Treats

COGNITIVE STIMULATION

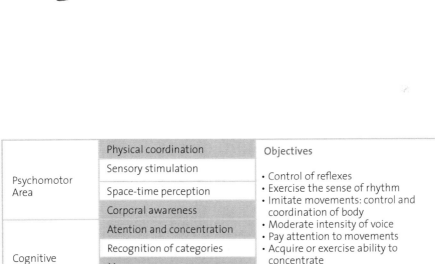

	Physical coordination	Objectives
Psychomotor Area	Sensory stimulation	• Control of reflexes
	Space-time perception	• Exercise the sense of rhythm
	Corporal awareness	• Imitate movements: control and coordination of body
Cognitive Area	Atention and concentration	• Moderate intensity of voice
	Recognition of categories	• Pay attention to movements
	Memory	• Acquire or exercise ability to concentrate
	Language and communication	• Acquire or exercise notion of colors
Social-emotional Area	Presentation	• Acquire or exercise notion of sizes
	Activity	• Develop or evaluate short-term memory
	Leave-taking and relaxation	• Stimulate socialization
	Board games	• Stimulate active listening
		• Explore different ways of communicating

149

The objective of this game is for the RI and the dog to dance following prompts provided on cards.

We lay out on a table two rows of paired cards. One card has the dog's action and the other has that to be performed by the RI.

Starting with the first pair, the RI tells the dog what he's supposed to do and stands by while he does it. Then he flips over the other card to see what he must do: jump up and down on one leg, make like he's flying, wave his arms, etc. It could also simply provide a verb, such as Sing, Laugh, Hug, Brush, or the like.

Then we can go through a series in which the dog performs his action and the RI performs the one of his own that goes with it.

Variations:

– Once all the actions have been performed, we can ask the RI to use his memory to connect a certain action by the dog to one of his own dance steps or actions. In this version, the dog does one of the steps or actions and the RI must remember which of his goes with that particular one and perform it.

– Instead of going one-by-one, we can have the dog perform a sequence of "steps," and the RI must recall and perform his own corresponding sequence. We can make an association between a kind of food or an item from a person's daily routine with an action performed by the RI and the dog.

– The RI chooses and item (or a card illustrating an item) that he wants to link to some interaction with the dog, for example: fish-petting, toothpaste-tell the dod to 'Sit'…

COMMANDS FOR THE DOG	MATERIALS
• Head down on card	• Dog skills cards
• Target a card	• People movements cards
• Various tricks or skills	• Cards containing verbs or actions

	Physical coordination	Objectives
Psychomotor Area	Sensory stimulation	• Exercise overall coordination
	Space-time perception	• Exercise balance • Exercise sense of right and left
	Corporal awareness	• Pay attention to instructions
Cognitive Area	Atention and concentration	• Pay attention to the movements • Acquire or exercise concentration
	Recognition of categories	• Develop or evaluate short-term memory
	Memory	• Stimulate the imagination
	Language and communication	• Improve language comprehension and expression
Social-emotional Area	Presentation	• Accept and follow rules for social interaction
	Activity	• Stimulate active listening
	Leave-taking and relaxation	• Experience the pleasure of laughter and movement
	Board games	

CLAPPING AS REWARD

The objective of this game is for the RI to pay attention to the dog's movements and be able to identify the commands given by the therapist.

We ask the RI how he likes to be congratulated when he does something well. We then explain that the dog likes to get a treat when it performs a certain task or demonstrates a skill. In this exercise, the reward will be accompanied by a clapping of hands or the sounding of a clicker.

The RI must pay close attention, and every time the dog does performs an action correctly, he claps his hands and then gives the dog a treat. We begin with simple static commands, then add to the mix dynamic commands and the following variations:

- The RI or the therapist gives a previously established command and the dog performs the action a certain number of times.

- The dog either obeys the command or does not.

- The dog performs the commanded action, but within a sequence of other actions.

Each time the RI claps, he gives the dog a treat.

Variations:

- The number of actions to be performed can be steadily increased. The dog ends up performing a kind of previously established choreography of actions, with the RI clapping with each successful execution. When the "dance" is over, the number of times the RI clapped is the number of treats to be given to the dog.

COMMANDS FOR THE DOG	MATERIALS
• Target	• Skills cards
• Up	• Treats
• Paw	• Clicker
• Sit	
• Speak	
• Beg	
• Down	
• Hide	

152

	Physical coordination	Objectives
Psychomotor Area	Sensory stimulation	• Exercise eye-movement coordination
	Space-time perception	• Exercise fine motor skills
	Corporal awareness	• Develop idea of body structure and anatomy
Cognitive Area	Atention and concentration	• Acquire or exercise notion of space and direction
	Recognition of categories	• Pay attention to movements of others
	Memory	
	Language and communication	• Acquire or exercise ability to concentrate
Social-emotional Area	Presentation	• Learn and respect rules
	Activity	• Encourage trust in others
	Leave-taking and relaxation	• Work with feelings
	Board games	

The objective of this game is for the RI to memorize a sequence of tricks or skills.

The dog will perform a certain number of tricks or actions while the RI observes him attentively.

The IP then gives the RI a stack of cards illustrating dog skills or tricks and the RI must put them in order in which the dog just performed them.

If the sequence is correct, the dog will repeat the actions as the RI "dictates" them. If there's a mistake in the sequence, the dog will not obey the mistaken command.

Variations:

– The dog's series of tricks or actions has a pre-established logical sequence that the RI is not privy to. When this series is performed, the RI must choose from the skills cards the actions he thinks will continue the series in the same vein. If his choice is correct, the dog will perform the commanded actions.

COMMANDS FOR THE DOG	MATERIALS
• Various tricks and skills	• Skills cards

Psychomotor Area	Physical coordination	Objectives
	Sensory stimulation	• Develop or evaluate visual memory
	Space-time perception	• Develop logical thinking
	Corporal awareness	
Cognitive Area	Atention and concentration	
	Recognition of categories	
	Memory	
	Language and communication	
Social-emotional Area	Presentation	
	Activity	
	Leave-taking and relaxation	
	Board games	

155

The objective of this game is for the RI to correctly impart orders so that the dog obeys them.

Using the deck of skills cards, we have him:

- describe what the dog on the card is doing
- imitate with his body that action
- say what the verbal order is
- demonstrate the hand-gesture command

The RI or the dog chooses a card and the IP provides a demonstration of how to impart the command both verbally and by gesture so the RI has a clear example of how to do it himself.

Following the IP's demonstration, the RI takes his position in front of the dog and must communicate with him. Special attention is paid to the individual's bearing, body language and tone of voice.

If he issues the order correctly, the IP will give the hand signal for that command to the dog.

If the RI's bearing or tone of voice is not appropriate, the IP gives the "No" gesture and the dog stays still.

COMMANDS FOR THE DOG	MATERIALS
• Stay	• Skills cards
• Give	• Treats
• Fetch	
• Mark	
• Various tricks	

COGNITIVE STIMULATION

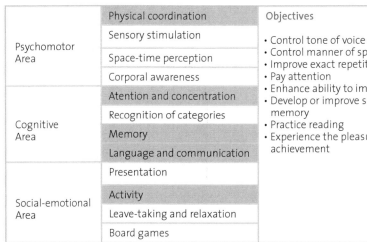

		Objectives
Psychomotor Area	Physical coordination	• Control tone of voice
	Sensory stimulation	• Control manner of speaking
	Space-time perception	• Improve exact repetition
	Corporal awareness	• Pay attention
Cognitive Area	Atention and concentration	• Enhance ability to imitate
	Recognition of categories	• Develop or improve short-term memory
	Memory	• Practice reading
	Language and communication	• Experience the pleasure of achievement
Social-emotional Area	Presentation	
	Activity	
	Leave-taking and relaxation	
	Board games	

157

WHAT DO THE HOOPS SAY?

The objective of this game is for the RI to obey the commands given to him by the dog.

We lay out for different colored hoops on the floor. Each one of them represents a certain action that the RI must perform.

We can use different ways to determine the color of hoop to proceed with:
Use the color die. Toss it, and the RI and dog go to the hoop of the color that comes up.

The dog, following the IP's signal, goes to a certain hoop. The RI follows him there without taking his eyes off him.

The dog takes the RI a colored card, a ball or a piece of fruit. The RI then goes with the dog to the hoop of that color.

At first, the IP, accompanied by the dog, will demonstrate the different actions that go with each hoop. The RI then will be asked to repeat it, with or without the help of the IP.

Then the dog proceeds to a particular hoop, sits there and waits for the RI to perform the corresponding action.

- Blue hoop: touch a certain part of the dog's body.
- Red hoop: command the dog to do a trick
- Green hoop: the RI must mime an activity or occupation
- Yellow hoop: answer a riddle posed by the therapist.

Variations:

- Each hoop represents a certain action to be performed or a challenge to be overcome by the RI.

COMMANDS FOR THE DOG	MATERIALS
• Sit	• Colored hoops
• Carry	• Color die
• Get it	• Actions cards
• Stay	• Riddle cards
• Yes	• Skills cards
✍	• Objects suitable for matching in pairs

158

		Objectives
Psychomotor Area	Physical coordination	• Exercise overall coordination
	Sensory stimulation	• Learn to lower voice
	Space-time perception	• Acquire or exercise ability to imitate
	Corporal awareness	• Develop or evaluate short-term memory
Cognitive Area	Atention and concentration	• Pay attention to instructions
	Recognition of categories	• Pay attention to movements of others
	Memory	• Acquire or exercise ability to concentrate
	Language and communication	• Develop or evaluate visual memory
Social-emotional Area	Presentation	• Enrich vocabulary
	Activity	• Experience the pleasure of movement
	Leave-taking and relaxation	
	Board games	

The objective of this game is to work with notions of space and sequential time.

The dog takes a series of hoops to the RI, who must place them around the room according to instructions given by the therapist, or a toss of the spatial indicator die, or from the dog, who selects a certain indicator card or marks one with his snout or paw.

When the RI correctly places a hoop, the dog performs a trick or earns a chip that will go toward a bigger reward previously agreed to between the therapist and the RI (chip economy).

Variations:

- The dog is situated in a certain place and the hoops must be placed in relationship to the dog's position. With each correct placement, the RI gets to give the dog a treat.

- Working with two dogs. The individual places the hoops according to instructions provided by the therapist.

COMMANDS FOR THE DOG	MATERIALS
• Get it	• Spatial indicator cards
	• Hoops
	• Chips

	Physical coordination	Objectives
Psychomotor Area	Sensory stimulation	• Gross motor skills
	Space-time perception	• Fine motor skills
	Corporal awareness	• Spatial orientation
	Atention and concentration	• Notion of axis of symmetry
Cognitive Area	Recognition of categories	• Attentiveness to instructions
	Memory	• Oral comprehension
	Language and communication	• Learning the dogs' names
Social-emotional Area	Presentation	• Pleasure of achievement
	Activity	• Notions of size
	Leave-taking and relaxation	
	Board games	

The objective of the game is to re-create the dog's daily activities using questions, deductions and photographs.

We have a series of photographs documenting things the dog routinely does over a 24-hour period.

We make from construction paper a time chart separating the day into its three main parts: morning, afternoon and night.

The RI asks questions and uses observation and deductive reasoning to determine which activities belong to which part of the day. He may receive help from his companions or from the IP.

Each time he correctly "places" an activity in it time-frame, the dog carries to him the photo of that activity and the RI attaches it to the chart.

The dog helps him by miming different activities or actions.

Variations:

– Photograph the activities of the RI's daily routine with the dog in the picture observing him. We can then use these photos in AAT to work on the sequence of activities in the daily life of people.

– Then we can draw parallels between the dog's schedule and the person's schedule.

COMMANDS FOR THE DOG	MATERIALS
• Stay • Give • Carry • Tricks and miming 	• Series of photos of the dog • Series of photos of the RI

		Objectives
Psychomotor Area	Physical coordination	• Work on tone of voice
	Sensory stimulation	• Work on modulating voice volume
	Space-time perception	• Develop symbolic thinking
	Corporal awareness	• Develop observational skills
Cognitive Area	Atention and concentration	• Stimulate the imagination
	Recognition of categories	• Improve language comprehension and expression
	Memory	• Improve pronunciation
	Language and communication	• Improve task planning
Social-emotional Area	Presentation	• Experience the pleasure of guessing right
	Activity	
	Leave-taking and relaxation	
	Board games	

PARTS IN SEQUENCE

The objective of this game is for the RI to memorize associations between numbers and parts of the dog's body.

We introduce the dog to the RI and explain that each part of the animal's body is going to be assigned a number. The RI touches a part of the dog's body and tosses the die. The dog retrieves it, and the number that came up is the one assigned to that body part.

The number of body parts assigned numbers varies according to the degree of difficulty we choose for the exercise. The dog is in the "stay" position.

The IP says a number and the RI touches the part of the dog's body assigned that number. If he's right, he gets to give the dog a treat.

Now the IP says two numbers and the RI must touch those parts in order. We increase the exercise's complexity by increasing the length of the sequence of numbers.

Variations:

- We lay out colored hoops on the floor. Each part of the dog's body corresponds to a color. The dog sits in a hoop, and the RI touches the part of the body associated with the hoop's color.

- The dog then sits in one, then another color hoop. The RI touches the corresponding body parts in order. The sequences then can be made longer and longer.

COMMANDS FOR THE DOG	MATERIALS
• Sit	• Numbered die
• Stay	• Body parts die
• Stand	• Colored hoops
• Get it	
✍	

COGNITIVE STIMULATION

	Physical coordination	Objectives
Psychomotor Area	Sensory stimulation	• Exercise fine motor skills
	Space-time perception	• Develop sense of body structure and anatomy
	Corporal awareness	• Codification and de-codification of symbols
Cognitive Area	Atention and concentration	• Develop or evaluate visual memory
	Recognition of categories	• Develop or evaluate short-term memory
	Memory	
	Language and communication	
Social-emotional Area	Presentation	
	Activity	
	Leave-taking and relaxation	
	Board games	

165

The objective is to engage in a relaxed activity aimed at identifying and remembering the parts of the dog's body.

The dog is lying on a table. We will identify each part of the body with a card. We give each RI a drawing of the outline of a dog with spaces in which to write the name of parts of the body.

The IP touches the various parts of the dog and the participants fill in the right word on the corresponding spaces on their drawing or stick on a label with the name.

Variations:

– The RI attaches the names of the parts directly to the dog's body.

– Mark a spot on the drawing of the dog. The RI must stick an adhesive label on that part of the live dog and another on the corresponding part of his own body or that of a companion.

– Spin the body parts roulette wheel, mark what comes up on the drawing and on the dog. Then write its function.

– The IP recites a sequence of various parts of the body, touching them or affixing a label to them.

– One by one, the RI must repeat the sequence in order and add another part at the end.

COMMANDS FOR THE DOG	MATERIALS
• Down • Stay	• Drawing of the outline of a dog • Wheel or die of body parts • Pencil • Glue • Adhesive labels of various colors • Body parts cards

		Objectives
Psychomotor Area	Physical coordination	
	Sensory stimulation	• Exercise fine motor skills
	Space-time perception	• Pay attention to the movements of others
	Corporal awareness	• Develop or evaluate visual memorty
Cognitive Area	Atention and concentration	• Develop or evaluate short-term memory
	Recognition of categories	• Recognize the parts of a whole
	Memory	• Practice reading
	Language and communication	• Improve language comprehension and expression
Social-emotional Area	Presentation	
	Activity	
	Leave-taking and relaxation	
	Board games	

HOOPS AND MEMORY

The objective of this game is for the RI to place hoops on the dog's body and then, as a reward, he gets to throw the dog the same number of balls as the hoops he has correctly placed.

With the dog standing in the "stay" position, the IP tells the RI where to place the hoop on the dog. The color, size and location of the hoops can vary: right, left, in front, in back, above, below... Or, he can show the RI a picture of a dog with hoops placed in a certain way and, after memorizing the information, the RI reproduces on a live dog the placement of hoops in the picture.

After this has been done, the RI must reproduce the same disposition of hoops on a second dog, one himself or on a companion.

We can increase the difficulty of the exercise by changing the position of the second dog in relation to that of the first.

For each correctly placed hoop, the RI earns a ball that will allow him to interact with the animal.

Each ball represents a command that the RI will give the dog before giving him a treat: "Sit," "Shake," "Down,"...

Then the RI tosses the ball. In a loud and clear voice he tells the dog to bring it back to him. He accepts the ball and, before giving the dog a treat, he gives him the correct command. If the dog obeys, he gives him a treat.

Attention must be paid to the RI's tone of voice and body language when communicating with the therapy dog.

To conclude the exercise, with the dog and the RI together, we review all the information provided and the degree of satisfaction achieved.

COMMANDS FOR THE DOG	MATERIALS
• Stay • Sit • Give • Fetch • Stand • Various tricks or skills 	• Different sized hoops • Colored hoops • Cards showing hoops on body • Balls

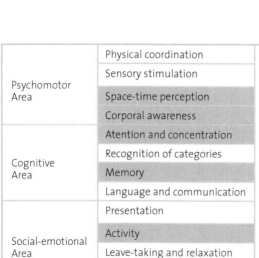

COGNITIVE STIMULATION

			Objectives
Psychomotor Area	Physical coordination		• Exercise memory • Practice executive actions • Exercise visual-space perception • Exercise sense of place in space • Exercise sense of left-right • Develop sense of body structure and anatomy • Pay attention to instructions • Improve oral comprehension • Experience the pleasure of achievement • Experience the pleasure of guessing correctly
	Sensory stimulation		
	Space-time perception		
	Corporal awareness		
Cognitive Area	Atention and concentration		
	Recognition of categories		
	Memory		
	Language and communication		
Social-emotional Area	Presentation		
	Activity		
	Leave-taking and relaxation		
	Board games		

The objective is for the RI to foster an affectionate relationship with the dog in the right way.

We show him that the dog, when given the command "kiss," gives us a kiss where we tell him to give it.

We show him how this is done several times, then propose to him that he tell the dog to give him a kiss on the arm, and then give him a treat.

We then toss the body parts die and the RI must give the dog a kiss on the part of the body that comes up.

He again asks the dog for a kiss, and gives him a treat.

The RI tosses the die again and now will give the dog a kiss on the same place he gave it before and on the place that came up on the second toss.

If he does this correctly, the dog gives the RI a kiss and the RI gives the dog a treat.

The game continues like this for as long as is deemed appropriate and useful.

COMMANDS FOR THE DOG

- Kiss
- Get it

MATERIALS

- Body parts die
- Treats

		Objectives
Psychomotor Area	Physical coordination	• Exercise sense of touch
	Sensory stimulation	• Develop or evaluate short-term memory
	Space-time perception	• Recogzine the parts of a whole
	Corporal awareness	• Develop language: comprehension and expression
Cognitive Area	Atention and concentration	• Stimulate physical interaction and physical contact
	Recognition of categories	
	Memory	
	Language and communication	
Social-emotional Area	Presentation	
	Activity	
	Leave-taking and relaxation	
	Board games	

The objective is for the RI to attach clips to the dog's coat and remove them, according to instructions from the IP.

We have clips of different colors or with different decorative motifs (animals, items of clothing, seasons of the year, etc.) that the RI can play with.

The dog lies down on his side. We attach clips to his coat along his back and on other parts of his body.

The IP asks the RI to remove a clip of a certain color or with a certain motif.

Variations:

– The RI tosses the body parts die and must attach a clip on the part that comes up.

– We ask the RI to place a clip of a certain color on a part of the body and then find the card illustrating that body part or explain its function.

– We can mark the clips with letters, then use them to write a message on the dog's coat.

– We can make a model of a dog with the clips the RI removes from the dog's coat.

– The RI can use each of the clips he removes to hold a treat and give it to the dog directly in the mouth.

COMMANDS FOR THE DOG	MATERIALS
• Down • Stay	• Colored clips • Numbered clips • Clips with letters or shapes • Different sized clips • Body parts die

		Objectives
Psychomotor Area	Physical coordination	• Exercise fine motor skills
	Sensory stimulation	• Exercise hand-eye coordination
	Space-time perception	• Develop sense of body structure and anatomy
	Corporal awareness	• Improve oral comprehension
Cognitive Area	Atention and concentration	• Acquire or exercise notion of numbers and quantity
	Recognition of categories	• Acquire or exercise notion of colors
	Memory	• Acquire or exercise notion of sizes
	Language and communication	• Acquire or exercise notion of geometric shapes
Social-emotional Area	Presentation	• Practice reading and writing
	Activity	• Categorize: form groups
	Leave-taking and relaxation	
	Board games	

The objective of this game is for the RI to place hoops on the dog's body. He is guided either by a photograph or by instructions from the IP.

We put the dog on a table and give the RI a die whose facets show a dog with hoops on different parts of his body.

The RI tosses the die and, looking at the photo that comes up, identifies the part of the body with the hoop.

He then touches that part of the dog on the table, names it and places the hoop.

This same game can be played by having a companion place the hoops on the RI's body, or by having the dog bring the hoops to the RI, who places them on himself.

Variations:

– Remembering sequences: Each time the die is tossed, the RI must remember the hooped parts that came up in previous throws and must again place all those hoops before positioning the one resulting from the latest toss.

– The color and size of the hoops can be varied.

– The RI must collect the hoops from different parts of the room by following spatial indications from the IP.

COMMANDS FOR THE DOG	MATERIALS
• Stand	• Colored hoops
• Stay	• Hoops of different sizes
• Carry	• Die showing hoops on
• Mark	body parts

	Physical coordination	Objectives
Psychomotor Area	Sensory stimulation	• Exercise overall dynamic coordination • Exercise sense of place in space • Exercise sense or left-right • Form a mental image of body structure and anatomy • Acquire or exercise ability to imitate • Improve oral comprehension • Enrich vocabulary • Stimulate physical contact and interaction
	Space-time perception	
	Corporal awareness	
Cognitive Area	Atention and concentration	
	Recognition of categories	
	Memory	
	Language and communication	
Social-emotional Area	Presentation	
	Activity	
	Leave-taking and relaxation	
	Board games	

CLIPS AND ACTIVITIES

The objective is for the RI to engage in a series of activities with the dog, depending on what color clip is drawn from different jars.

Before beginning the game, we assign a different colored clip to several activities that RI likes to do with the dog.

Then we fill four good-sized jars with different materials, such as: water, sand, rice, cream, cooking oil, etc. We put a different colored clip into each jar.

Taking turns, each RI puts his hand in a jar and withdraws the clip. He must say what activity goes with that color clip, and if he is correct, he gets to do that with the dog; brush him, toss him a ball, take a walk, teach him a trick, etc.

As the game progresses, the IP can ask the RI whose turn it is what color clips have already been withdrawn or what the activities were that preceded his turn.

Variations:

– The task is to make a collar for the dog with wooden beads of different shape and color. We can group the beads by shape or by color or by shape and color. The RI tosses the color die or the shape die and, depending on what come up, the appropriate bead is withdrawn from one of the jars and used to fashion the collar.

– The dog will bring the RI a colored ball. The color of the ball determines which jar the RI should reach into.

COMMANDS FOR THE DOG	MATERIALS
• Fetch	• Colored clips
• Give	• Activities cards
• Carry	• Jars
• Stand	• Materials for filling jars
	• Colored wooden beads for making collar
	• Beads of different geometric shapes
	• Colored balls

COGNITIVE STIMULATION

		Objectives
Psychomotor Area	Physical coordination	• Exercise sense of touch
	Sensory stimulation	• Exercise fine motor skills
	Space-time perception	• Develop or evaluate visual memory
	Corporal awareness	• Follow norms for social interaction
Cognitive Area	Atention and concentration	• Association: Stimulate cooperation in a group
	Recognition of categories	• Stimulate short-term memory
	Memory	• Reduce reluctance to touch certain materials
	Language and communication	
Social-emotional Area	Presentation	
	Activity	
	Leave-taking and relaxation	
	Board games	

The objective of the exercise is to play a game of dominoes between the therapist and the RI, with the help of the dog.

On one side of the room, the wooden domino tiles, the dog and his technician. On the other side of the room are the RI and the therapist, each one with some tiles on the playing table.

The game begins with the RI telling his partner – the dog – which tile he wants to put into play.

The dog selects a tile and takes it to the RI either in a basket or in his mouth. The RI looks to see if it is the tile he asked for. If it is, he places it in play. If it is not, he informs the dog in a friendly way of the mistake, and holds on to the tile to use later in the game.

Variations:

- The domino tiles can have numbers or be of different colors or shapes.

- The game is played between the RI and the dog, in which case it is played on the floor.

- Each of the players, one accompanied by the therapist and one by the technician, has his own tiles and says which one they wish to put into play. If needed, help can be provided by the partner.

COMMANDS FOR THE DOG	MATERIALS
• Sit	• Domino tiles
• Stay	• Basket
• Come	
• Fetch	
• Give	
• Mark	
• Get it	

COGNITIVE STIMULATION

		Objectives
Psychomotor Area	Physical coordination	• Exercise hand-eye coordination
	Sensory stimulation	• Pay attention to instructions
	Space-time perception	• Improve oral comprehension
	Corporal awareness	• Acquire or exercise notion of numbers
Cognitive Area	Atention and concentration	• Acquire or exercise notion of colors
	Recognition of categories	• Acquire or exercise notion of geometric shapes
	Memory	• Develop or evaluate visual memory
	Language and communication	• Learn to respect social norms
Social-emotional Area	Presentation	• Cooperation: Stimulate helpful relationships
	Activity	
	Leave-taking and relaxation	
	Board games	

THE MUSICIANS OF CTAC

The objective of this game is for the RIs to compose a song using sounds made by animals.

Sitting in a circle, we show the RIs a series of cones or colored handkerchiefs, under each of which is hidden a card with a picture of an animal and a number.

Taking turns and accompanied by the dog, each RI must locate the cone corresponding to an animal chosen by his companions.

The RI lifts the cone or the handkerchief and the dog picks up the card.

If it is the right animal, he looks at the hidden number and gives the dog that many treats. If he is wrong, the dog barks.

After each person takes his turn, we review the locations of the animals cone by cone, imitating the sound they make.

Then the dog, following a command, stops at a certain cone. The participants make the corresponding animal's sound in chorus. A sequence of stops by the dog at different cones makes for a song sung together by all the RIs.

Lastly, the dog sits beside a certain cone and the RI who first shouts out the correct animal for that cone gets to be the first one to pet the dog when the group takes its leave.

COMMANDS FOR THE DOG	MATERIALS
• Heel	• Cones or colored handkerchiefs
• Fetch	• Cards showing animals or
• Give	animal figurines
• Stay	• Treats
• Target	• Numbered tiles or chips
• Speak	
• Treat	

180

		Objectives
Psychomotor Area	Physical coordination	• Exercise hearing and rhythm • Pay attention to instructions • Acquire or exercise symbolic thinking • Develop or evaluate: auditory memory visual memory short-term memory • Stimulate creativity • Stimulate the imagination • Develop pre-verbal language • Develop language comprehension and expression • Stimulate group interaction and communication • Learn and respect social norms
	Sensory stimulation	
	Space-time perception	
	Corporal awareness	
Cognitive Area	Atention and concentration	
	Recognition of categories	
	Memory	
	Language and communication	
Social-emotional Area	Presentation	
	Activity	
	Leave-taking and relaxation	
	Board games	

The objective of this game is for the RI to memorize a sequence performed by the dog and then repeat it, with or without the animal.

We lay out a grid on the floor with whatever we want to work with: numbers, colors, shapes, names, skills, etc.

The dog walks through the layout, sitting at certain points according to commands. The speed of the steps in the sequence can be varied according to the RI's capabilities.

The RI must then reproduce the sequence, walking to the same points in the layout in the same order they were visited by the dog.

Variations:

– Create the sequence along a line of colored hoops. In each hoop, the dog will perform a certain trick or skill illustrated in a photograph. The RI memorizes the color of the hoop of that particular action. Then we turn the photos face down and the RI commands the dog to perform the correct action in each hoop. We can change the order of the hoops, and ask the RI to again have the dog perform the trick or skill corresponding to each hoop's color.

– Associate certain actions with colors. Do something with the dog depending on the color of the hoop or cone: petting, brushing, give a treat, touch a certain part of the body, etc. Then we can determine a new sequence by tossing the colors die. The RI and the dog perform the series of actions following the order established by throwing the die.

COMMANDS FOR THE DOG	MATERIALS
• Sit	• Colored cones
• Target	• Colored hoops
• Skills and tricks	• Brushes
	• 4x4 grids with different kinds of objects to work with

		Objectives
Psychomotor Area	Physical coordination	• Develop or evaluate visual memory
	Sensory stimulation	• Develop or evaluate short-term memory
	Space-time perception	• Develop ability to observe
	Corporal awareness	• Exercise overall dynamic coordination
Cognitive Area	Atention and concentration	• Pay attention to movements of others
	Recognition of categories	• Acquire or exercise ability to imitate
	Memory	• Accept norms of social interaction
	Language and communication	
Social-emotional Area	Presentation	
	Activity	
	Leave-taking and relaxation	
	Board games	

183

The objective is for the RI to reproduce actions performed by his companions.

We place the dog in front of a group alongside a basket full of toys and tools to be used for interacting with him; balls, hoops, brushes, water bowl, food bowl, collar, leash, etc.

We divide the group into pairs of RIs who, taking turns, approach the dog. The first one addresses the dog, saying his name in a loud and clear voice. He chooses an item from the basket and engages in the corresponding activity with the dog.

Then his partner approaches the dog, introducing himself. He now takes the same item his partner used and performs the same action his partner did while facing the group. The group decides whether the imitation was satisfactory. If it is, both members of the pair get to give the dog treats.

Variations:

– We make a circle. Taking turns, a participant approaches the dog and imitates, in the correct order, the actions performed previously by his companions. Then he adds another action to the sequence. Then he returns to his place and selects another participant to work with the dog. This person goes to the center of the circle and repeats in the correct order the actions, naming each one, performed by those who preceded him.

COMMANDS FOR THE DOG	MATERIALS
• Stay • Sit • Treat • Appropriate skills and tricks	• Dog grooming items • Dog toys

		Objectives
Psychomotor Area	Physical coordination	• Pay attention to movements of others
	Sensory stimulation	
	Space-time perception	• Acquire or exercise ability to imitate
	Corporal awareness	• Develop or evaluate visual memory
Cognitive Area	Atention and concentration	• Develop ability to observe
	Recognition of categories	• Stimulate socialization
	Memory	
	Language and communication	
Social-emotional Area	Presentation	
	Activity	
	Leave-taking and relaxation	
	Board games	

COGNITIVE STIMULATION

The objective of this game is for the RI to match socks in correct pairs.

We use two baskets, each one of which has one sock from a pair.

The dog takes the RI a sock from one of the baskets and the RI must find its mate in the other basket before the dog completes a previously determined circuit.

If he succeeds, he gets to give the dog the treat hidden in the second sock.

Finally, when all the socks have been matched up, the RI will put them on the dog according to instructions given by the IP, such as: the red ones on the front paws, etc.

Variations:

– The RI has a pile of single unmatched socks. In order to earn each one's mate, he must perform a series of tasks or correctly follow instructions from the IP: provide the right answer to a question, complete a circuit, have the dog do a trick. When he has earned the socks to form all the pairs, he gets to put the socks on the dog.

– We lay out several single unmatched socks along the dog's back. The RI is given another single sock and he must find its mate on the dog's back and lay the one he was given on it to form the pair.

COMMANDS FOR THE DOG	MATERIALS
• Fetch	• Socks of different lengths
• Down	• Socks of different colors
• Stay	• Socks of different textures
• Drop	• Socks with different patterns
	• Baskets

		Objectives
Psychomotor Area	Physical coordination	• Exercise fine motor skills • Develop idea of body structure and anatomy • Exercise notion of right-left • Pay attention to instructions • Acquire or exercise notion of colors • Acquire or exercise notion of sizes • Link or match objects • Recognize properties of objects • Experience the pleasure of achievement
	Sensory stimulation	
	Space-time perception	
	Corporal awareness	
Cognitive Area	Atention and concentration	
	Recognition of categories	
	Memory	
	Language and communication	
Social-emotional Area	Presentation	
	Activity	
	Leave-taking and relaxation	
	Board games	

The object of this game is to make a collar of different colored pieces to put around the dog's neck.

We give the RI a basket filled with different colored pieces. The dog sits down at a certain bowl or bucket, the color of which will tell the RI which pieces he should remove from his basket, with the help of the IP if needed.

The RI then puts those pieces in the bucket where the dog has sat down. Once the RI has separated all the pieces according to color in the various bowls or buckets, he can begin making the collar by taking a piece whose shape is indicated to him by the dog.

The dog will indicate the shape he wants by:

- sitting down at a hoop holding a card showing that shape
- taking the RI the geometric shapes die
- touching his snout or paw to a particular card among an array on the wall.

Now, with all the "beads" of the right shape and color, the RI will string them.

He can ask the dog to help him by pulling the end of the string once he has put it through the hole. Lastly, he puts the collar around the dog's neck.

Variations:

– We give the RI a drawing showing the sequence of beads for the collar. The person must tell the dog one-by-one which pieces he needs and the animal fetches them. If he brings the correct one, he deposits it in a basket.

– The same exercise can be done using things from everyday life that can be strung together. This version allows us to work with activities of the daily routine.

COMMANDS FOR THE DOG	MATERIALS
• Mark on the wall • Get it • Sit at distance • Fetch • Down • Throw	• Items that can be strung, of different shapes and colors • Everyday objects that can be strung • Colored hoops and bowls • Cards illustrating geometric shapes • Geometric shapes die

	Physical coordination	Objectives
Psychomotor Area	Sensory stimulation	• Exercise visual perception: depth, background and figure
	Space-time perception	• Acquire or exercise notion of colors
	Corporal awareness	• Acquire or exercise notion of geometric shapes
Cognitive Area	Atention and concentration	• Exercise hand-eye coordination
	Recognition of categories	• Develop social interaction
	Memory	• Enhance self-esteem
	Language and communication	
Social-emotional Area	Presentation	
	Activity	
	Leave-taking and relaxation	
	Board games	

The object of this exercise is for the RI to classify strands of wool by color and length.

We get ready to play by cutting strands of different colored wool into various lengths. With the dog lying on a table, we place the strands over and under his body.

The RIs must take turns selecting a strand and group them according to color and length. When all the strands have been classified, they can be used to make a collage.

Variations:

– Find the strands on the part of the dog's body indicated by the IP.

– Find them according to color, either indicated by the IP or by tossing the colors die.

– The degree of visibility of the strands can be varied according to the therapy session's goals.

– We can hid drawings of bones of differing color and size. The RIs find them using observation and their sense of touch.

– Cards showing everyday items or figurines can be hidden.

– Treats can be hidden.

– We can hid pieces of a puzzle. The RI gets to put it together once he has found all the pieces.

COMMANDS FOR THE DOG	MATERIALS
• Down	• Table
• Stay	• Spools of wool of different colors
	• Scissors
	• Construction paper
	• Objects for hiding

		Objectives
Psychomotor Area	Physical coordination	
	Sensory stimulation	• Exercise hand-eye coordination
	Space-time perception	• Exercise sense of touch • Develop sense of body structure
	Corporal awareness	• Acquire or exercise notion of colors • Acquire or exercise notion of sizes
Cognitive Area	Atention and concentration	• Recognizer parts of a whole
	Recognition of categories	• Improve language comprehension and expression
	Memory	• Stimulate group communication and interaction
	Language and communication	• Learn and follow social norms
Social-emotional Area	Presentation	
	Activity	
	Leave-taking and relaxation	
	Board games	

The objective of this game is for the RI to feed the dog according to the dog's size.

We place four different colored hoops on the floor and put a number in each one.

Each hoop is the house of a large or small toy dog.

The RI tosses the colors die or spins the colors wheel. Whatever color comes up, the RI looks into that color hoop, sees what number is there and takes that many treats.

The treats are given to the therapy dog that most resembles the toy dog in that hoop.

Variations:

- We can change the game by associating each hoop with:
    - names
    - adverbs
    - verbs
    - other sizes
    - arithmetic concepts: results of mathematical operations

- The IP indicates a certain hoop. The RI approaches him and takes the number of treats corresponding to the number in that hoop and gives them to the dog representing the agreed upon association (the one named "Spot," the fastest one, etc.).

COMMANDS FOR THE DOG	MATERIALS
• Sit	• Hoops
• Stay	• Colors die
• Treat	• Numbered die
	• Treats

192

	Physical coordination	Objectives
Psychomotor Area	Sensory stimulation	• Improve oral comprehension
	Space-time perception	• Acquire or exercise notions of numbers and quantity
	Corporal awareness	• Acquire or exercise notion of colors
Cognitive Area	Atention and concentration	• Acquire or exercise notion of sizes • Acquire or exercise notion of geometric shapes
	Recognition of categories	
	Memory	• Establish relationships or associations between objects
	Language and communication	• Recognize properties of objects • Acquire notions of arithmetic
Social-emotional Area	Presentation	
	Activity	
	Leave-taking and relaxation	
	Board games	

COGNITIVE STIMULATION

KEEPING CLEAN

The objective of this exercise is to work on the RI's daily grooming and hygienic habits by considering those of the dog.

The IP introduces the activity. He explains that there are things the dog cannot do by himself, and that he needs our help. If we do them for him, then why wouldn't we do them for ourselves?

We look at cards illustrating grooming habits of a dog, and those of people: bathing, combing or brushing hair, brushing teeth, cutting fingernails, washing the face.

Once we decide on what aspect of grooming or hygiene to work on, the dog, following instructions from the RI, collects the appropriate tools.

After that, he brings from a basket the items the RI needs for his own personal hygiene.

Variations:

– The dog decides, by indicating a card or a hoop, what grooming habit he wants to engage in with the RI.

– The RI tosses the body parts die and, depending on what comes up, says what grooming habit is the right one for that area.

COMMANDS FOR THE DOG	MATERIALS
• Sit	• Dog grooming tools
• Down	• Personal hygiene items
• Bang	• Body parts die
• Stay	• Colored hoops
• Teeth	• Colors die
• Get it	• Illustrative cards

194

		Objectives
Psychomotor Area	Physical coordination	• Exercise overall dynamic coordination
	Sensory stimulation	• Stimulate sensory perception
	Space-time perception	• Encourage getting into a routine
	Corporal awareness	• Enhance self-respect and self-esteem
Cognitive Area	Atention and concentration	• Improve task planning
	Recognition of categories	• Develop or evaluate visual memory
	Memory	
	Language and communication	
Social-emotional Area	Presentation	
	Activity	
	Leave-taking and relaxation	
	Board games	

The objective of this game is for the RI to develop the habit of feeding the dog a healthy diet.

The RI must identify the ingredients used in preparing the dog's meal. In order to be able to do that, we explain the process involved in making dog food, and the RI must indentify or guess the relevant products.

The RI must be aware of the fact that each dog has its own nutritional needs, as well as a portion size that must be respected.

First, the RI tells the dog to sit, and to wait (stay). Then, as the dog watches attentively, he prepares the meal. When it's ready, he tells the dog to come and eat.

If we want the RI to do this at home with his family's pet, we can draw up a chart showing the feeding schedule and amounts.

Depending upon the amount of involvement we're looking for, we can ask the RI to closely observe how the dog eats so that he might, for example, use a spoon to feed him or feed him by hand one croquette at a time.

Variations:

– If we have a group of dogs to work with, we can identify each one with a color, and by name. We toss the color die, and the RI must feed the dog whose color came up, but only after saying his name.

COMMANDS FOR THE DOG	MATERIALS
• Sit	• Vegetables
• Stay	• Rice
• Come	• Chicken
	• Water
	• Dry dog food
	• Bowls
	• Measuring cup

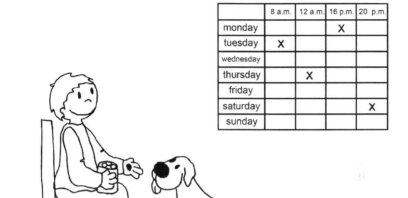

	8 a.m.	12 a.m.	16 p.m.	20 p.m.
monday			X	
tuesday	X			
wednesday				
thursday		X		
friday				
saturday				X
sunday				

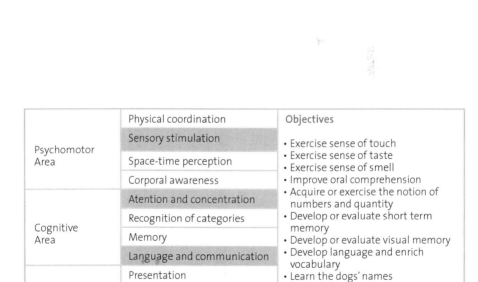

Psychomotor Area	Physical coordination	Objectives
	Sensory stimulation	• Exercise sense of touch
	Space-time perception	• Exercise sense of taste
	Corporal awareness	• Exercise sense of smell
Cognitive Area	Atention and concentration	• Improve oral comprehension
	Recognition of categories	• Acquire or exercise the notion of numbers and quantity
	Memory	• Develop or evaluate short term memory
	Language and communication	• Develop or evaluate visual memory
Social-emotional Area	Presentation	• Develop language and enrich vocabulary
	Activity	• Learn the dogs' names
	Leave-taking and relaxation	• Learn and respect social norms
	Board games	

197

The objective of this game is to work with concepts of space in relation to the dog.

First, we play a game of imitation. The RI must assume a position in relation to an object that replicates the position of the dog in relation to the same object. For example, if the dog is on a table, the RI must get up on a table. He can, if so desired, say out loud the instruction while he is carrying it out.

Then, using drawings if they're deemed helpful, we ask the RI to place the dog at different points in the room: under the table or on top of it, in front of or behind a chair. If he performs the action correctly, the RI wins a treat that he can give the dog after the animal does a trick or performs a skill. Here we can also introduce the idea of "chip economy." Each time the RI accumulates a certain number of successful actions (for each one of which he gets a chip), the dog will perform a skill.

Next, the dog will show the RI a card. He can either carry it to him in his mouth, or let the RI withdraw it from a pocket on the animal's CTAC Dog Blanket.

The RI must then quickly put himself in the position indicated by the card in relation to a certain object in the room (for example, far from the table, or under it), or far from the dog.

Variations:

– Involve more than one RI in the game as a way of improving communication among the participants.

– Use more than one dog in order to improve powers of discrimination.

– Have the RI assume the same posture as the dog and facing in the same direction.

– Tell a story that includes concepts of positions in space. As the IP narrates, the RI changes the dog's position by using the appropriate commands.

– Place hoops on the dog's body, using the relevant CTAC illustrative cards.

COMMANDS FOR THE DOG	MATERIALS
• Stand	• Psycho-motor skills accessories
• Sit	• Hoops
• Stay	• CTAC dog blanket
•Various tricks and skills	• CTAC illustrative hoops cards

		Objectives
Psychomotor Area	Physical coordination	• Exercise hand-eye coordination
	Sensory stimulation	• Exercise visual-space perception
	Space-time perception	• Exercise sense of place in space
	Corporal awareness	• Develop mental image of body structure
Cognitive Area	Atention and concentration	• Acquire or exercise notions of space and direction
	Recognition of categories	• Acquire or exercise ability to imitate
	Memory	• Develop or evaluate short-term memory
	Language and communication	• Develop powers of observation
Social-emotional Area	Presentation	• Foment helpful relationships
	Activity	• Experience the pleasure of achievement
	Leave-taking and relaxation	
	Board games	

MANY-COLORED CLOTHES

The objective of this game is to identify different kinds of clothing and work on the process of getting dressed.

We ask the RI to place a series of balloons differentiated by color, shape or written numbers on the floor. The IP then puts a piece of attire of either the RI or the dog next to each of the balloons. The RI withdraws from the pockets on the CTAC dog blanket one or several cards telling him which number, color or shape balloon he should send the dog to retrieve the piece of clothing. If the dog does not have a CTAC blanket, the IP can hold out a fan of cards for the RI to pick from.

When the dog reaches the correct spot, the RI congratulates him. The dog picks up the piece of clothing and takes it to the RI. He says out loud the name of the item, then repeats the process until all the pieces of clothing have been retrieved.

Lastly, the individual to whom the clothing belongs (either the dog or a RI) puts on the clothes (or is dressed) following the correct order of getting dressed.

Variations:

– Distinguish between the dog's "clothing" and the RI's own.

– Differentiate between items of clothing according to the weather or season.

COMMANDS FOR THE DOG	MATERIALS
• Fetch • Carry • Give • Stay • Stand • Get it • Down • Drop	• Various types of clothing • Various types of closing mechanisms (zippers, buttons, etc.) • Signal items (balloons, cones, numbers, shapes) • CTAC dog blanket • Decks of cards

		Objectives
Psychomotor Area	Physical coordination	• Exercise visual-motor coordination
	Sensory stimulation	• Exercise hand-eye coordination
	Space-time perception	• Exercise sense of touch
	Corporal awareness	• Develop mental image of body structure
Cognitive Area	Atention and concentration	• Develop and control muscular strength
	Recognition of categories	• Identify objects
	Memory	• Develop symbolic thinking
	Language and communication	• Stimulate the imagination
Social-emotional Area	Presentation	• Enrich vocabulary • Form groups according to characteristics
	Activity	• Stimulate group communication and interaction
	Leave-taking and relaxation	• Experience the pleasure of achievement
	Board games	

The objective of this game is for the RI to learn to handle different kinds of closure mechanisms on clothing in order to be able to dress himself.

The dog takes the RI several items of clothing with different closing mechanisms (buttons, zippers, Velcro, etc.) The RI takes each one and examines it with his eyes and fingers, memorizing the type of closure on each of the pieces. He then lays them out on the floor in a line, in a way that the closures are not visible.

Then he takes a card showing a particular closing mechanism from a pocket on the CTAC dog blanket, or selects one from an array offered by the IP. He now must remember, and point out, the piece of clothing with that type of closure.

The exercise continues until each piece of clothing is paired with one of the cards.

Variations:

– We place cones to form a circuit in the room. We have several CTAC psycho-motor leashes upon which are drawn different kinds of clothing closure mechanisms.

– The IP shows the RI a sequence of cards illustrating different types of closures. The RI must memorize the sequence, for example: buckle, zipper, Velcro.

– The RI walks the dog along the circuit of cones. At each one, he unhooks and leaves the leash he was using on the dog and selects from the various leashes deposited at that cone the one corresponding to the next closure in the sequence.

COMMANDS FOR THE DOG	MATERIALS
• Give • Get it • Fetch • Carry • Stand	• Clothes with different closing mechanisms • Cards illustrating different closures

COGNITIVE STIMULATION

		Objectives
Psychomotor Area	Physical coordination	• Acquire or exercise symbolic thinking
	Sensory stimulation	• Acquire or exercise ability to concentrate
	Space-time perception	• Develop or evaluate visual memory
	Corporal awareness	• Develop language: comprehension and expression
Cognitive Area	Atention and concentration	• Distinguish between parts of a whole
	Recognition of categories	• Establish relationships between objects
	Memory	• Recognize characteristics of objects
	Language and communication	
Social-emotional Area	Presentation	
	Activity	
	Leave-taking and relaxation	
	Board games	

The objective of this exercise is for the RI's to interact among themselves while learning to remember a brief routine.

The RI's form a circle with at least a few steps of space between each other. The technician walks the dog clockwise around the circle, greeting each one out loud so that the names of all participants are clearly stated.

Taking turns, the RI takes the leash and walks the dog along the circles inside perimeter until he reaches a companion, with whom he will have a brief conversation before handing over the dog.

The subject matter of the talk can vary according to the session's objectives: introducing themselves, or the dog; an exchange of commonplaces about how the person looks; comments about what we know he or she is good at; about their personality or behavior.

When the exchange is over, RI1 gives the dog to RI2 and goes back to his spot, while RI2 moves on to the next companion, talks a bit, and so on around the circle.

Variations:

– We attach a very long cord to the dog and the RIs remain in their spots. The dog goes from one to the other, encircling each one, which prompt exclamations and conversation among them. When the dog is finished, they are all connected – "caught" – in the net.

– The RIs toss a big ball from one to another, with the dog chasing it.

COMMANDS FOR THE DOG	MATERIALS
• Stay	• Leash
• Get it	
• Stand	
• Heel	

COGNITIVE STIMULATION

		Objectives
Psychomotor Area	Physical coordination	
	Sensory stimulation	• Develop social interaction
	Space-time perception	• Stimulate group interaction and communication
	Corporal awareness	• Learn to respect social norms.
Cognitive Area	Atention and concentration	• Stimulate active listening • Listening without interrupting
	Recognition of categories	• Foment affinitive relationships
	Memory	• Experience the shedding of inhibitions
	Language and communication	• Establish a ritual framework for introductions and greetings
Social-emotional Area	Presentation	• Foment sense of fairness by affording all equal time
	Activity	
	Leave-taking and relaxation	
	Board games	

The objective of this activity is to draw large cards bearing the name of each RI to facilitate communication among all the session's participants. It also fosters easier interaction between the AIT and the participants, as it allows him or her to address each individual by name.

Before beginning the session, each RI identifies himself by writing his name beside a drawing of a dog, on a sheet with a template for coloring, next to a drawing of themselves, or simply on an oversized blank card.

Then the RI and the technician will make a sort of "license plate" identifying the dog, a bone-shaped sign that the session's participants will decorate while the AIT introduces the dog to them and encourages the first interaction.

They can receive articles for decorating the plate directly from the dog (carrying items in his mouth). Another way to foment interaction between the RIs and the animal would be to hide some pencils or markers under the dog in repose, or have the dog carry a basket containing art supplies (construction paper, foam rubber, markers, rollers, etc.) to those who call him.

Variations:

– Each participant writes some of his or her positive qualities on their ID card.

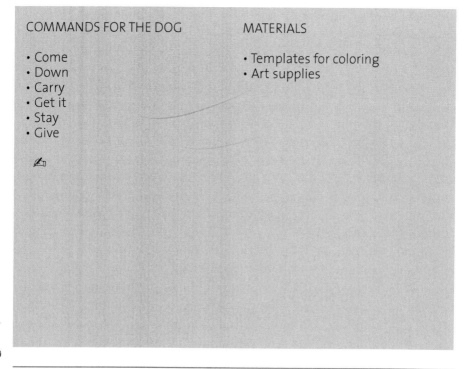

COMMANDS FOR THE DOG

• Come
• Down
• Carry
• Get it
• Stay
• Give

MATERIALS

• Templates for coloring
• Art supplies

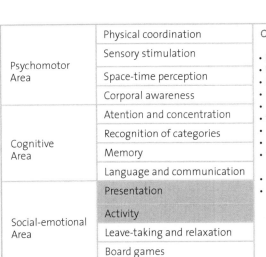

		Objectives
Psychomotor Area	Physical coordination	
	Sensory stimulation	• Reinforce self-esteem
	Space-time perception	• Promote self-awareness
	Corporal awareness	• Become aware of one's capabilities
Cognitive Area	Atention and concentration	• Learn to express interest in others
	Recognition of categories	• Learn people's names
	Memory	• Stimulate socialization
	Language and communication	• Learn introductions
Social-emotional Area	Presentation	• Learn to respect social norms
	Activity	• Stimulate group communication
	Leave-taking and relaxation	and interaction
	Board games	• Exercise fine-motor skills

Objectives:
• Reinforce self-esteem
• Promote self-awareness
• Become aware of one's capabilities
• Learn to express interest in others
• Learn people's names
• Stimulate socialization
• Learn introductions
• Learn to respect social norms
• Stimulate group communication and interaction
• Exercise fine-motor skills
• Exercise hand-eye coordination

The objective of this exercise is for the RI to maneuver around a grid with the dog, following a "map."

We draw a four-by-four grid on the floor, one that exhibits 16 boxes, which can be marked with large dots or mushrooms. We prepare several oversized cards showing the grid and, by connecting the dots in the boxes, chart different routes of varying degrees of difficulty.

The dog takes one of the cards to the RI, who examines it attentively for a few moments. He then walks that particular route on the grid on the floor, with the dog looking on. When he completes his pathway, he engages in some sort of interaction with the dog.

Then he goes back the same way he came, following the route backwards. At the starting point, he gives the dog a treat.

To make the task easier, the RI can be allowed to carry the route card with him as he goes.

Variations:

– The RI guides the dog along the grid toward the route's destination point. He does this by giving verbal instructions to the dog such as: two blocks to the right, one block down, three blocks to the left, etc.

COMMANDS FOR THE DOG	MATERIALS
• Heel	• Cards showing routes
• Give	• 16 mushrooms or adhesives to
• Carry	mark the grid
• Various tricks and skills	• Skills cards

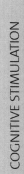

COGNITIVE STIMULATION

		Objectives
Psychomotor Area	Physical coordination	• Exercise visual-space perception
	Sensory stimulation	• Exercise eye-motor coordination
	Space-time perception	• Develop or evaluate visual memory
	Corporal awareness	• Learn to respect rules and norms
Cognitive Area	Atention and concentration	• Learn to make decisions
	Recognition of categories	• Learn to accept making mistakes
	Memory	• Improve decision-making capabilities
	Language and communication	
Social-emotional Area	Presentation	
	Activity	
	Leave-taking and relaxation	
	Board games	

DOG ARITHMETIC

The objective of this activity is to motivate the RI to perform simple arithmetic.

There are several fun ways to involve the dog in this:

– Representation of sums and remainders: The RI places the correct number of hoops around the neck of the dog as a result of the operation proposed by the IP. For example: The IP asks, "How much is 3+5?" The RI should answer, "Eight." Then he drapes eight hoops over the dog's head. The IP asks him to subtract two from the previous result. The RI says, "Six," and removes two hoops. The IP tells him to add four. The RI makes the calculation, and places four more hoops on the dog. Lastly, he counts the ten hoops around the dog's neck.

– Giving treats: the RI will give the dog the number of treats resulting from the operation that comes up on a toss of the mathematical dice. We use the treats to represent the result of various operations of addition and subtraction.

– Gymkhana of operations: we can "hide" mathematical operations along a psycho-motor circuit that the RI will complete with the dog. At each cone, the RI finds an operation, the solving of which gives way to a certain trick or action he must perform with the dog.

– Addition and subtraction walk: the RI must arrive at a finish line walking in a straight line with the dog. He advances the number of paces resulting from an addition, and he steps backwards the number of paces resulting from a subtraction.

– We can have the dog express the result of an addition or subtraction by barking that many times, and the RI says whether the number of barks is correct.

COMMANDS FOR THE DOG	MATERIALS
• Watch	• Cones
• Sit	• Hoops
• Stay	
• Speak	
• Various tricks and skills	

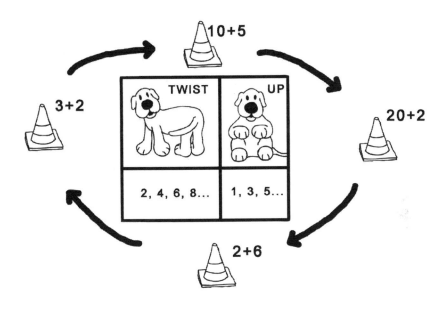

		Objectives
Psychomotor Area	Physical coordination	• Pay attention to instructions
	Sensory stimulation	• Acquire or exercise notion of numbers and quantity
	Space-time perception	• Visually recognize numbers
	Corporal awareness	• Establish relationships between objects
Cognitive Area	Atention and concentration	• Acquire basics of arithmetic: adding and subtracting
	Recognition of categories	• Learn to listen and respond
	Memory	• Experience the pleasure of achievement
	Language and communication	• Learn to make decisions
Social-emotional Area	Presentation	• Learn to accept one's mistakes
	Activity	• Learn to come up with solutions for problems
	Leave-taking and relaxation	
	Board games	

THE DOG'S SEQUENCE

The objective of this activity is for the RI to continue a sequence of actions begun by the dog.

We lay out across the floor a certain number of either colored chips, numbers, geometric shapes, trick cards or everyday objects.

The dog, accompanied by the AIT, moves from one to another (perhaps sitting on each chip or card) in a certain order, establishing a sequence.

The RI closely observes the dog's movements, which are repeated. When the dog interrupts the sequence at a certain point, the RI must continue the sequence.

Variations:

– We put adhesive shapes or colors on the dog's back, and the RI must continue placing the right adhesives for completing the sequence.

– We have the dog in the "stay" position and the IP establishes a sequence of body parts by gently touching each part. Then the RI reproduces the sequence.

COMMANDS FOR THE DOG	MATERIALS
• Sit • Stay • Get it 	• Chips with letters, shapes or numbers • Adhesives of different shapes and colors

212

	Physical coordination	Objectives
Psychomotor Area	Sensory stimulation	• Pay attention to the movements of others
	Space-time perception	• Acquire or exercise ability to concentrate
	Corporal awareness	• Acquire or exercise the ability to pay attention
Cognitive Area	Atention and concentration	• Develop or evaluate short-term memory
	Recognition of categories	• Develop or evaluate visual-space perception
	Memory	• Experience the pleasure of achievement
	Language and communication	
Social-emotional Area	Presentation	
	Activity	
	Leave-taking and relaxation	
	Board games	

COGNITIVE STIMULATION

THE PARTS OF THE BODY

The objective of this activity is for the RI to learn the different parts of the dog's body in order to be able to identify them both on a live dog and in a drawing, as well as relate them to the parts of his own body.

With the dog resting comfortably beside the RI, the AIT names each of the parts of the dog's body. He does this going from the larger areas to the smaller, more detailed and specific parts. We ask the RI to touch and pet the different parts. After a while, we ask him to touch a certain part of his own body, then the corresponding part on the dog. Lastly, he tosses the body-parts die (either human or canine), identifies which part came up, then touches that part on himself or the dog.

Variations:

– We lay out a circuit with colored cones, leaving in each one a piece of a puzzle of the human body and a card with a dog trick or skill. The RI spins the color wheel or tosses the color die. He then goes to that-colored cone and has the dog do the trick on the card there. The dog then gives him the piece of the puzzle, which the RI identifies, points it out on his own body and on that of the dog, and lastly fits it into the puzzle.

– We bandage parts of the body of either the dog or the RI.

– We place a certain number of colored adhesives on the dog's body. The RI closely examines the dog, then, without looking at the animal, select cards showing the body parts marked with an adhesive.

COMMANDS FOR THE DOG	MATERIALS
• Sit • Down • Stay • Stand	• Interactive die • CTAC cards of parts of dog's body • CTAC cards of parts of human body

214

			Objectives
Psychomotor Area	Physical coordination		• Exercise the sense of touch
	Sensory stimulation		• Exercise sense of left-right
	Space-time perception		• Develop mental image of body structure
	Corporal awareness		• Pay attention to instructions
Cognitive Area	Atention and concentration		• Acquire or exercise ability to imitate
	Recognition of categories		• Establish relationships between objects
	Memory		• Stimulate active listening
	Language and communication		• Enhance recognition by touch
Social-emotional Area	Presentation		
	Activity		
	Leave-taking and relaxation		
	Board games		

The objective of this activity is for the RI to move, from one side of a "path" to the other, the items needed to perform a certain task with the dog.

We lay out a path of hoops, either in a straight line, two parallel lines, or in two asymmetrical lines in order to help the RI work with the notion of asymmetrical modes of locomotion (walking and running) and symmetrical ones (jumping with feet together.)

At one end of the pathway we place the dog, who has clearly made a request: "I want you to clean me," or "I want you to feed me," "I want to go for a walk with you," etc. The RI is at the path's other end, where there are cards illustrating different objects.

With the IP's help, the RI chooses the cards showing the items he needs to carry out the task requested by the dog, and he states the sequence in which they are used in performing it.

To get the actual item illustrated on the card, he must ask the IP for it by name. Upon receiving it, he follows the path of hoops to reach the dog.

When he has all the elements he needs beside the dog, the RI again describes the correct sequence for carrying out the action.

Variations:

- Dress the dog according the season: the dog chooses the time of year and the RI must select the cards showing the appropriate clothing. He then exchanges the cards for the real items of clothing, and puts them correctly on the dog.

COMMANDS FOR THE DOG	MATERIALS
• Heel	• Hoops
• Treat	• Activities cards
• Stay	• Cards showing items of canine
• Sit	care
• Speak	
• Get it	

	Physical coordination	Objectives
Psychomotor Area	Sensory stimulation	• Exercise overall dynamic coordination
	Space-time perception	• Exercise hand-eye coordination
	Corporal awareness	• Improve balance
Cognitive Area	Atention and concentration	• Form mental representation of a situation
	Recognition of categories	• Recognize objects
	Memory	• Improve task planning
	Language and communication	• Develop social interaction
Social-emotional Area	Presentation	• Become aware of one's capabilities and limitations
	Activity	• Learn to make decisions
	Leave-taking and relaxation	• Mitigate shyness and withdrawal
	Board games	

REMEMBERING HANDKERCHIEFS

The objective of this activity is for the RI to recall the outfit worn by one of the dogs and recreate the exact outfit on another.

The AIT introduces the RI to a dog, and shows him a bag full of colored kerchiefs. This activity can also be done with colored clips, rubber bands or adhesives.

With or without help, the RI "disguises" the dog, then observes him closely in order to memorize the placement of each of the handkerchiefs.

Then the RI goes to another dog and, from memory, dresses him just like the first one.

He compares the two dogs. For each of the elements of the outfit duplicated correctly, he gets a treat to be given to the dog in exchange for a trick.

Variations:

– Another fun way of doing this is by using socks. We put four different socks on one dog, and give the mates to the RI for him to put on another dog in the same arrangement.

– One RI puts a kerchief of a certain color on a part of his dog's body, and a companion RI watches in order to be able to place a kerchief of the same color on the same part of his dog.

COMMANDS FOR THE DOG	MATERIALS
• Sit	• Handkerchiefs
• Down	• Socks
• Stay	• Adhesives

		Objectives
Psychomotor Area	Physical coordination	• Exercise fine motor skills
	Sensory stimulation	• Exercise sense of left-right
	Space-time perception	• Develop mental image of body structure
	Corporal awareness	• Acquire or exercise ability to imitate
Cognitive Area	Atention and concentration	• Develop or evaluate short-term memory
	Recognition of categories	• Develop or evaluate long-term memory
	Memory	• Develop ability to observe
	Language and communication	• Accept norms of social interaction
Social-emotional Area	Presentation	• Exercise sight-body coordination
	Activity	• Positive resolution of conflicts
	Leave-taking and relaxation	• Learn to plan
	Board games	

The objective of this activity is for the RI to count different things.

The dog and his world is a rich source of things for counting:

– The number of times he barks
– The number of parts of his body
– The number of treats he gets
– The number of teats she has in one row or both
– The number of brush strokes we make in one direction (with the lay of the coat)
– The number of strokes in the other direction (against the lay)
– The number of times he performs a certain trick (e.g. twist to the right)
– The number of balls he brings us from a basket
– The number of hoops the RI places over his head

The dog performs skills required by each game: does tricks, brings balls, shows her belly, etc.

COMMANDS FOR THE DOG	MATERIALS
• Give	Depending on the game:
• Treat	
• Speak	• Treats
• Roll over	• Bowls with treats
• Down	• Hoops
• Beg	
• Carry	

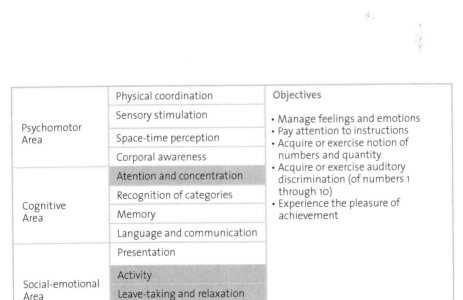

		Objectives
Psychomotor Area	Physical coordination	• Manage feelings and emotions
	Sensory stimulation	• Pay attention to instructions
	Space-time perception	• Acquire or exercise notion of numbers and quantity
	Corporal awareness	• Acquire or exercise auditory discrimination (of numbers 1 through 10)
Cognitive Area	Atention and concentration	• Experience the pleasure of achievement
	Recognition of categories	
	Memory	
	Language and communication	
Social-emotional Area	Presentation	
	Activity	
	Leave-taking and relaxation	
	Board games	

The objective of this activity is for the RI to perform certain actions previously decided upon by the IP.

– Verbs

The AIT introduces his four dogs and associates each one with a certain color. Taking turns, the RIs spin the color wheel or toss the colors die. The RI says the name of the dog whose color came up, and goes to him. He pets the animal until he finds hidden in its coat a card with a verb written on it, and then does that action.

– Shapes

We place different geometric shapes on the floor or stick them on the wall, and associate each one with a verb or an action. The dog either sits on a given shape, or touches it with his paw or snout, and the RI must perform the action associated with that shape.

– What's missing?

Each dog has an oversized card with an incomplete drawing of a dog. (If there's only one dog, the activity is done with the dog pointing out different cards spread out on the floor or stuck to the wall.) When the dog signals a certain card (by sitting on it or touching it), the RI must observe that card and touch the part of the dog that is missing in that drawing. If he is correct, the RI turns the card over to find a trick or skill he has the dog perform.

COMMANDS FOR THE DOG	MATERIALS
• Sit • Get it 	• Verb cards • Cards with incomplete drawings of dogs

COGNITIVE STIMULATION

		Objectives
Psychomotor Area	Physical coordination	• Develop mental image of body structure
	Sensory stimulation	• Acquire or exercise symbolic thinking
	Space-time perception	• Recognize parts of a whole
	Corporal awareness	• Detect the absence of an essential part of the whole
Cognitive Area	Atention and concentration	• Improve verbal and non-verbal communication
	Recognition of categories	• Increase tolerance of frustration
	Memory	• Develop use of symbols: codification and de-codification
	Language and communication	• Express feelings
Social-emotional Area	Presentation	• Experience the shedding of inhibition
	Activity	
	Leave-taking and relaxation	
	Board games	

THE HANGMAN TRICK

The objective of this game is for the RI to discover a "hidden" command, and have the dog perform the corresponding trick or skill.

At the beginning of the session, each RI is given a card showing a certain trick. The RIs then describe the picture on their card and the AIT demonstrates how each command is given, both verbally and by gesture.

The RIs practice giving their command to the therapy dog. If more than one dog is available, the technician asks the RI which one he prefers to work with, and what kind of treat he wants to give him if he performs well.

After the practice session, an RI goes to the blackboard and decides which dog he will use, and what trick he wants that dog to do, but he does NOT reveal his choices. Let's say he wants to use the dog named "Cuca," and wants her to "Sit." So the command is, "Cuca, sit!"

This gives us the phrase for our game of "Hangman."

He draws on the blackboard a horizontal line for each of this letters in the phrase. (In this case, that would be 7 lines.)

Now the other RIs, taking turns, call out letters. The one directing the game puts the correct letters in the spaces, and adds something to the "hanged man" drawing for each incorrect one.

Once the phrase, and thus the dog and the trick, is guessed, the RI at the blackboard decides which of his or her companions will have the dog perform the trick. If that person does this correctly, the RI at the blackboard congratulates him or her.

That person then remains at the blackboard to decide on a dog and a trick, and another game begins.

COMMANDS FOR THE DOG	MATERIALS
• Various tricks and skills	• Blackboard
• Sit	• Skills cards
• Stay	
• Treat	
• Watch	

COGNITIVE STIMULATION

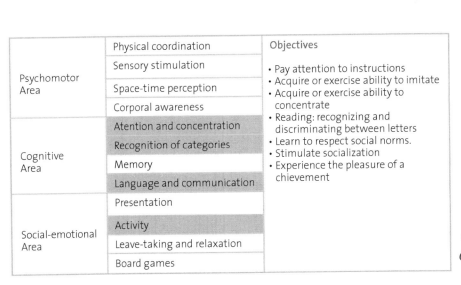

		Objectives
Psychomotor Area	Physical coordination	• Pay attention to instructions • Acquire or exercise ability to imitate • Acquire or exercise ability to concentrate • Reading: recognizing and discriminating between letters • Learn to respect social norms. • Stimulate socialization • Experience the pleasure of a chievement
	Sensory stimulation	
	Space-time perception	
	Corporal awareness	
Cognitive Area	Atention and concentration	
	Recognition of categories	
	Memory	
	Language and communication	
Social-emotional Area	Presentation	
	Activity	
	Leave-taking and relaxation	
	Board games	

The objective of this game is for the RIs to "buddy-up" in pairs for participation in a subsequent activity.

The activity begins with the RIs dividing into two groups, each with the same number of participants.

The AIT and a dog take their place between the two groups, and the technician describes in detail the animal's characteristics:

Height: short, medium, tall
Build: lean, medium, robust
Length and color of coat
Hair type: straight, wavy, kinky
Ear shape: standing or floppy, V-shaped or U-shaped
Tail: length and position
Angle of forehead (the stop)
Eye shape and color
Snout: pug (short), medium, long

Then each RI gets a photograph of a dog. The therapy dog circulates, and when he stops in front of a participant, that person must describe, in a voice that can be heard by all, the dog in his picture.

Whoever among the other participants has a picture of a dog similar to the one being described calls the therapy dog and gives him the photo. The dog takes it to the RI giving the description, who compares the two pictures to determine if indeed the dogs look alike. If they do, those two RIs become "partners."

Variations:

– Match up canine emotions and their human counterparts

– Match up facial expressions and emotions

COMMANDS FOR THE DOG	MATERIALS
• Fetch	• Cards illustrating dog breeds
• Stay	
• Get it	
• Give	
• Heel	
• Stand	

	Physical coordination	Objectives
Psychomotor Area	Sensory stimulation	• Encourage paying attention and focus
	Space-time perception	• Increase observational ability
	Corporal awareness	• Develop descriptive ability
Cognitive Area	Atention and concentration	• Exercise listening to and observing each participant, respecting the other's turn and refraining from interruption
	Recognition of categories	• Identification of physical attributes
	Memory	• Improve verbal comprehension and expression
	Language and communication	
Social-emotional Area	Presentation	
	Activity	
	Leave-taking and relaxation	
	Board games	

The objective of this activity is for the RI to imitate the actions of another participant.

The RIs form a semi-circle, with a dog standing before them. Nearby are implements the RIs can use to interact with the dog: brushes, balls, moist towelettes, skills cards, etc.

An individual volunteers to go first. He goes to the dog and touches it, looks it over, pets it, gives it a kiss, makes a face or a gesture, stands on tiptoes, etc.

Then another RI steps forward, goes to the dog and does the same things the previous person did, only adding a new one at the end. A third RI then goes through the entire sequence of the first two, and tacks on his own move. And so on, until all have taken their turn.

Variations:

– The dog "says" what he wants each RI to express in their respective turns: Who am I? What am I? What do I like? What bothers me?, etc. The IP has made up oversized cards with these and other questions and either taped them to the wall or spread them out on the floor. The AIT directs the dog to one or another of the cards in order to pose the questions to the RI.

COMMANDS FOR THE DOG	MATERIALS
• Sit	• Balls
• Stay	• Bowls
• Treat	• Treats
• Various tricks and skills	• Skills cards
• Get it	

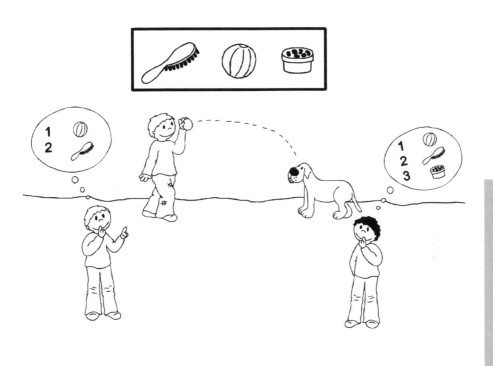

	Physical coordination	Objectives
Psychomotor Area	Sensory stimulation	• Exercise fine motor skills • Pay attention to the movements of others • Develop or evaluate visual memory • Develop or evaluate short-term memory • Recognize the characteristics of objects • Develop observational ability • Stimulate the imagination • Explore different forms of communication • Stimulate group communication and interaction • Experience the shedding of inhibitions
	Space-time perception	
	Corporal awareness	
Cognitive Area	Atention and concentration	
	Recognition of categories	
	Memory	
	Language and communication	
Social-emotional Area	Presentation	
	Activity	
	Leave-taking and relaxation	
	Board games	

The objective of this activity is for the RI to communicate – by various means – what he wants to do with the dog. We're seeking to increase motivation to the point that it facilitates communication.

– Pointing out the object: The RI will initiate an activity with the dog using an object such as a ball, a brush, hoops or treats. To be able to play with the dog, the RI must point out with his finger the item designated by the IP. He can be physically assisted if necessary. Once the RI has pointed out the objects he wants to use, the IP holds out two of them for the RI to choose from.

– Pointing out or handing over a card: The RI indicates to the IP what he wants to do with the dog by touching or handing over a card showing that activity, or he places the card on the dog's breast.

– Association with pressed button: If the RI is able to activate a button or switch, we can associate a positive or negative concept, in conjunction with the dog, with a buzzer or light resulting from the push of a button.

– Alternative communication notebook: We can expand the RI's individual communication notebook with images relating to animal assisted activities: pronouns, verbs, actions, complements, etc. and in so doing enrich communication during the session.

Variations:

– The dog points out an object so that the RI pays attention and engages in the activity suggested by the dog.

– The IP points out an object for the RI to give the dog.

COMMANDS FOR THE DOG	MATERIALS
• Sit • Stay • Mark • Watch • Various tricks and skills 	• Cards showing dog accessories • Dog accessories: leashes, collars, balls, etc.

COGNITIVE STIMULATION

		Objectives
Psychomotor Area	Physical coordination	• Pay attention to instructions
	Sensory stimulation	• Acquire or exercise symbolic thinking
	Space-time perception	• Acquire or exercise ability to concentrate
	Corporal awareness	• Establish relationships between objects
Cognitive Area	Atention and concentration	• Recognize the characteristics of objects
	Recognition of categories	• Develop symbolic function
	Memory	• Develop language: comprehension and expression
	Language and communication	• Learn and respect social norms
Social-emotional Area	Presentation	• Express feelings
	Activity	• Develop ability to self-motivate
	Leave-taking and relaxation	
	Board games	

The objective of this activity is for the RI to interact with the dog through use of a story.

We choose an appropriate book for the individual RI, then create an ambience favoring maximum rapport between the RI and the dog. We try to arrange the participants so that the dog too can look at the book and so the RI can touch the dog. The possibilities include:

– The RI is seated in a chair, with the book resting on the table. The dog, seated at his side, can rest his head on the table, or he can be lying on the table with his head above the book.

– The RI is seated on the floor with the dog between him and the IP. The dog rests his head in the lap of the RI while he turns the pages of the book.

– The RI sits beside the dog and reads him the book.

The RI can...

– ...listen: the RI pets or touches the dog while listening to the IP read.
– ...read: the RI reads the story while the dog looks attentively at the book's pages.
– ...answer: the RI answers questions asked by the dog by way of cards.

Variations:

– After reading a story, a circuit is set up. As the RI answers questions posed by the IP about what happened in the story, he may proceed along the course beside the dog.

COMMANDS FOR THE DOG	MATERIALS
• Stay	• Book
• Head down	• Question cards
• Down	
• Look	
✍	

		Objectives
Psychomotor Area	Physical coordination	• Acquire or exercise ability to concentrate
	Sensory stimulation	• Improve oral comprehension
	Space-time perception	• Enrich vocabulary
	Corporal awareness	• Improve reading
Cognitive Area	Atention and concentration	• Learn to listen and respond
	Recognition of categories	• Enhance verbal expression
	Memory	• Create an affective bond
	Language and communication	• Develop capacity to enjoy good feelings
Social-emotional Area	Presentation	
	Activity	
	Leave-taking and relaxation	
	Board games	

The objective of this activity is for the RIs to pay attention to what their companions are doing so they can answer the IP's questions and interact with the dog.

We place the dog on a table at one end of the room. In order to approach him, the RIs must proceed along one of three thematic trails: the collar trail, the brush trail, or the dog anatomy trail.

The collar trail: The RI will advance along a trail of colored hoops. At its end, he will find some strings with colored beads strung on them. He must pick out the one with the colors aligned in the same order as that of the hoops he has just traversed.

Brush trail: On a circuit set up with box (like those used in step gymnastics), the RI will find various brushes. He must choose the one indicated, either by way of physical description or description of location, by the AIT. Then he will use it to brush the dog.

Dog anatomy trail: The RI will proceed along a zig-zag circuit of cones. Each cone will have a CTAC card illustrating a canine body part that the RI must remember so as to be able to touch, in order, each of those parts of the dog's body.

Variations:

– On the collar trail, give the RI a specific sequence of colors. The RI then lays out the hoops in the correct order on his way to the dog. When he arrives, he will attach colored adhesives in the same sequence on the dog's coat.

– Complete each circuit so as to be able to dress up the dog with clothing or kerchiefs.

COMMANDS FOR THE DOG	MATERIALS
• Down	• Large table
• Stay	• Colored hoops
	• Strings with colored beads
	• Step boxes
	• Brushes
	• Cones
	• Cards illustrating dog body parts

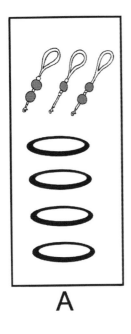
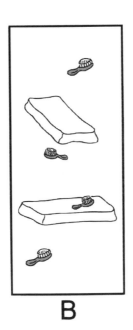
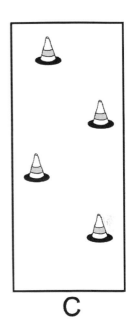

A   **B**   **C**

COGNITIVE STIMULATION

		Objectives
Psychomotor Area	Physical coordination	• Exercise gross motor skills
	Sensory stimulation	• Exercise hand-eye coordination
	Space-time perception	• Exercise tactile perception
	Corporal awareness	• Develop sense of anatomy
Cognitive Area	Atention and concentration	• Pay attention to movements of others
	Recognition of categories	• Acquire or exercise capacity for concentration
	Memory	• Develop or evaluate short-term memory
	Language and communication	• Cooperation: Stimulate helpful relationships
Social-emotional Area	Presentation	• Learn to respect social norms
	Activity	• Experience the pleasure of achievement
	Leave-taking and relaxation	• Experience the pleasure of laughter
	Board games	

The objective of this activity is for the RI to interact with the dog according to the number and color of bowling pins he knocks over.

The IP and the RI together determine what color bowling pin corresponds to which part of the dog's body.

After solving a riddle, answering a question or guessing the meaning of a mimed action presented by one of his companions – in the event of group activity – the dog delivers a ball to the RI. With the dog observing closely, the RI throws the ball in an effort to knock over the greatest number of bowling pins.

On the one hand, the number of pins knocked over determines the number of treats the RI can give the dog; on the other, the colors of the fallen pins determine which parts of the dog's body the RI can pet or brush.

Variations:

– The pins represent tricks or abilities that the RI can command the dog to perform. After each trick, the RI gives the animal a treat.

– The pins represent actions that the RI must perform with one of his companions.

– Each pin represents an item of clothing that the RI will put on the dog; knocking over all six pins wins a complete disguise.

COMMANDS FOR THE DOG	MATERIALS
• Fetch	• Colored bowling pins
• Give	• Balls
• Stay	• Brush
	• Riddles

		Objectives
Psychomotor Area	Physical coordination	• Exercise hand-eye coordination
	Sensory stimulation	• Develop sense of anatomy
	Space-time perception	• Develop aim: precision
	Corporal awareness	• Pay attention to instructions
Cognitive Area	Atention and concentration	• Establish relationships between different objects
	Recognition of categories	• Promote good group dynamics
	Memory	• Explore different forms of communication: mime, rhythmic, figurative, theatrical
	Language and communication	• Develop or evaluate visual memory
Social-emotional Area	Presentation	• Experience the pleasure of laughter
	Activity	
	Leave-taking and relaxation	
	Board games	

The objective of this game is for the RI to teach the dog to touch an object with his snout.

Teaching the dog to perform a certain action is a good way for the RI himself to better comprehend the difficulty of teaching and learning new things, even if they seem simple.

For this activity we need two dogs: one that knows a certain skill and another that does not (or one that is sufficiently well-trained and obedient so as to stop short, on command, of completing the demonstration of that skill even though he knows it.)

We place an object in the middle of the room. The AIT gives the command "Cone," so that the dog goes to the cone or other object, touches it with his snout and immediately returns to the technician's side.

Each RI will experience how easy it is to give a command to an already-trained dog and see it followed. But then they see how complicated it is to teach an untrained animal to do the same thing. We must show him how to do it.

One way to proceed is to reward the dog for partial progress toward the goal, a technique known as successive approximations.

The RI learns to use the clicker to reinforce each of the dog's small steps toward the ultimate objective, which is to touch the object with his snout.

We emphasize throughout this exercise the importance of always employing respect and patience when teaching any behavior or skill.

COMMANDS FOR THE DOG	MATERIALS
• Mark • Cone • Get it	• Cone or other object

COGNITIVE STIMULATION

		Objectives
Psychomotor Area	Physical coordination	• Create an affective bond
	Sensory stimulation	• Pay attention to movements of others
	Space-time perception	• Acquire or exercise the capacity to concentrate
	Corporal awareness	• Learn and respect social norms
Cognitive Area	Atention and concentration	• Experience the pleasure of achievement
	Recognition of categories	• Develop an appropriate and positive self-image
	Memory	• Learn to make decisions
	Language and communication	• Set attainable goals
Social-emotional Area	Presentation	• Develop problem-solving abilities
	Activity	• Learn self-control
	Leave-taking and relaxation	• Learn to plan
	Board games	

The objective of this activity is to teach the RI the importance of the dog's tail in its interactions with humans and animals, and to learn to interpret its movements and positions. We play a game of questions and treats (for tricks), describing and matching up situations, and placing the tail on an illustration of a tail-less dog according to its mood or emotions.

It's easy to see how a dog feels by looking at the movement of its tail. Dogs move their tails to communicate socially; when they are alone, they don't do it, even if they are enjoying what they are doing.

What's the tail for?
• To communicate, and to disperse the dog's particular scent.
• It is an essential part of the dog's system of balance, much like a rudder.

What do the different positions and movements of the tail mean?

Lateral movement: Dogs often make a broad sweeping movement of the tail ("wagging") while playing or when they anticipate that something good is about to happen; they also employ this movement to redistributed their weight, or in preparation for attack.

High and flagging: The tail raised high and moved forward and back indicates the dog is in a good mood. The movement's speed will increase if they get what they want.

Horizontal: When a dog holds its tail horizontal to the ground or floor, it is interested in something.

Tail between its legs: A dog that is submissive, anxious or afraid will fold its tail between its legs. The more the tail is hidden, the more intense the emotion being felt.

Raised and rigid: A dog intent on asserting its authority often raises its tail slightly above the horizontal line. If it is provoked or angered by the perception of imminent aggression, it will further raise the tail and hold it fixed there.

Low and wagging: A tail held lower than horizontal with a slight back-and-forth motion indicates sadness, worry, insecurity, or can mean that the dog is ill.

COMMANDS FOR THE DOG	MATERIALS
• Get it • Stay • Carry • Steady tail	• Card illustrating dog without tail • Drawings of tails in different positions • "Feelings" die

	Physical coordination	Objectives
Psychomotor Area	Sensory stimulation	• Improve oral communication
	Space-time perception	• Acquire or exercise the ability to imitate
	Corporal awareness	• Stimulate creativity: other ways of thinking
Cognitive Area	Atention and concentration	• Develop the skill of observation
	Recognition of categories	• Enrich vocabulary
	Memory	• Cooperation: Encourage helpful relationships
	Language and communication	• Listening without interruptions
Social-emotional Area	Presentation	• Explore different means of communication
	Activity	• Expression of personality
	Leave-taking and relaxation	• Managing emotions and feelings
	Board games	

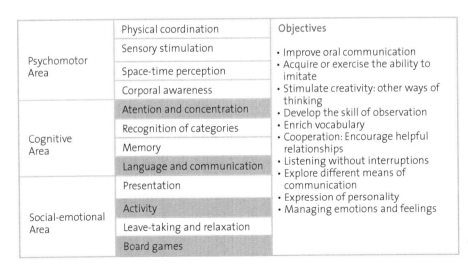

Dogs use all their facial features to deliver a range of messages. Let's look at several examples:

a) Ears: Canine ears are very mobile. They can turn and incline both forward and backward, which makes them very expressive. When the ears are slanted forward, the dog is alert. When they are back, he is relaxed; pricked-up ears indicate aggression and ears folded back fear, but with the possibility of aggression.

b) Eyes: A sweet and tender look in the eyes of a dog indicates affection and trust. A fixed and impatient look expresses interest and alertness; a look that's askew or oblique conveys submission or insecurity. Rapid blinking is a reaction to stress. Direct and sustained visual contact sends a message of domination and aggression.

c) Brow: If the skin on the brow is relaxed then the dog is, too. If it is smooth but taut, tugged slightly backward, he is afraid or feeling aggressive. When he is anxious, he furrows his brow, just like people do.

d) Mouth: A relaxed dog holds his mouth partially open. A panting dog might be nervous, stressed or simply hot. If he licks the snout of another dog or the face of a person, it is a form of greeting or a sign of submission, although some dogs lick to calm themselves or relax. If the jaw is trembling, the dog expects something exciting to happen.

e) Lips: Relaxed lips indicate the dog is calm. A stressed dog pulls his lips back and wrinkles the corners of his mouth.

Exercise 1: We have a good-sized image of a human face and another of a dog's face in which the features (mouth, ears, etc.) – of which we have examples conveying different moods or emotions – can be interchanged. The game consists of assembling a collage of the face according to a particular emotion or a hypothetical situation.

Exercise 2: Identify the appropriate emotion evoked by a situation described by the IP.

COMMANDS FOR THE DOG	MATERIALS
• Carry • Drop • Stay • Sit • Get it	• Images of canine and human faces • "Feelings" die • Cards depicting situations

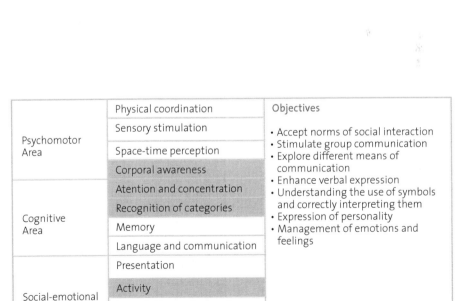

		Objectives
Psychomotor Area	Physical coordination	• Accept norms of social interaction
	Sensory stimulation	• Stimulate group communication
	Space-time perception	• Explore different means of communication
	Corporal awareness	• Enhance verbal expression
Cognitive Area	Atention and concentration	• Understanding the use of symbols and correctly interpreting them
	Recognition of categories	• Expression of personality
	Memory	• Management of emotions and feelings
	Language and communication	
Social-emotional Area	Presentation	
	Activity	
	Leave-taking and relaxation	
	Board games	

Dogs show us they are...

– Happy, calm and relaxed: They relax their ears and let them fall. The head is held neither high nor low and the brow is smooth. The corners of the mouth are relaxed, almost as if he's about to laugh. The tail is stationary or moving only slightly.

– Interested and alert: All the body parts are raised and inclined forward. The head is raised and the mouth is held slightly open. The eyes have an alert expression.

– Playful or excited: When a dog wants to play he lowers the front part of the body and raises the rump so the back bows, with the tail wagging rapidly. If his invitation to play is accepted, he will leap and bark to express his joy.

– Bored or sad: Generally, they will be stretched out on the floor with the head resting on the paws, the tail relaxed, ears down and a vacant look in the eyes.

– Submissive: The dog tries to look smaller than he is. They crouch or shrink in fear, with the back bowed and the head down or hidden. To demonstrate complete submission, a dog will roll onto its back and expose its belly.

– Dominant or aggressive: The whole body is raised and inclined forward so as to appear larger, stronger and more formidable. They stand on the tips of the paws and the hair on the nape and shoulders becomes erect. The tail is held high and fixed.

– **Exercise 1:** The RI is asked questions about how he thinks the dog feels in a certain situation, and how he himself would feel in that same situation. What would he suggest might be done to make the dog feel differently. What does he think could provoke in the dog a certain emotion, and what is it that causes that same emotion in him.

– **Exercise 2:** Imitate the different postures exhibited by the dog.

COMMANDS FOR THE DOG	MATERIALS
• Get it • Belly • Speak • Crawl • Curtsy • Look	• Die of canine emotions • Deck of situation cards • Cards of affective situations

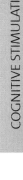

		Objectives
Psychomotor Area	Physical coordination	• Develop the capacity to connect to others' emotions
	Sensory stimulation	
	Space-time perception	• Develop capacity for empathy
	Corporal awareness	• Expression of emotions and feelings
Cognitive Area	Atention and concentration	• Verbal and non-verbal communication
	Recognition of categories	• Develop the capacity to enjoy positive feelings
	Memory	• Express fantasies and feelings
	Language and communication	
Social-emotional Area	Presentation	
	Activity	
	Leave-taking and relaxation	
	Board games	

COLLECTING BY CATEGORY

We spread haphazardly around the floor a certain number of objects belonging to the same family, such as animals (stuffed or plastic) and mix in objects from other groups or families, such as vehicles or fruits.

The RI will walk around the room accompanied by the dog, which can be on or off the leash and will have a basket in his mouth. When the RI stops at an object, the dog will sit and wait for him to place it in the basket. When the RI finishes his collection, the dog will lay down before him (without offering contact so as to avoid distraction) and observe the things the RI and the IP take from the basket. When an object of the chosen category is extracted, the RI gives it to the dog, who carries it to a chair and places it there, after which he receives a treat.

When all the objects of the desired category have been placed on the chair, the RI gets to command the dog to perform a skill.

Variations:

– The RI stands before a hoop inside which have been placed objects of different families. Behind that hoop are laid out the same number of hoops as families represented inside the foremost hoop. Each of the rearward hoops represents a family, such as fruits, vehicles, articles of clothing, etc.

The RI watches to see at which hoop the dog sits, then selects from the foremost hoop an object pertaining to the family represented by that hoop. If the object selected by the RI indeed belongs to that category, the dog goes to the RI to be given the object for deposit in the appropriate hoop.

– Separate by shape and size different types of dry dog food, then give the dog only that of a particular shape and size.

COMMANDS FOR THE DOG	MATERIALS
• Sit • Down • Heel • Carry • Fetch • Drop • Get it	• Objects of different categories • A basket comfortable for the dog to carry: one he will not trip over and that is not broad enough to bother his stride

		Objectives
Psychomotor Area	Physical coordination	• Exercise gross motor skills
	Sensory stimulation	• Exercise fine motor skills
	Space-time perception	• Encourage changing of body posture
	Corporal awareness	• Develop manual dexterity in picking up and placing
Cognitive Area	Atention and concentration	• Acquire or exercise sense of space and direction
	Recognition of categories	• Establish relationships between objects
	Memory	• Recognize characteristics of objects
	Language and communication	• Separate by characteristics: form groups
Social-emotional Area	Presentation	• Experience the pleasure of achievement
	Activity	
	Leave-taking and relaxation	
	Board games	

The objective of this activity is for the RI to identify cards illustrating canine-related objects and place them on a drawing of a dog.

We place in the center of the room a basket full of balls of primary colors. On the RI's command, the dog goes to the basket, takes one of the balls from it and carries it to the RI.

The IP will now hold up an object, and the RI must select the card showing that object that is the same color as the ball the dog just delivered to him. For example, if the IP held up a brush and the ball the RI got from the dog is red, then the RI must choose the card showing the red brush. Also, the RI can be asked to select the card showing an object that complements the one held up by the IP (while at all times respecting the color code), e.g.; if the IP has exhibited dog food, then the RI selects the card showing a bowl; if he holds up a fistful of hair, the RI selects the brush; a collar, then the leash, etc.

After naming the object and describing how it is used with the dog, the RI and the dog go together to place the card on the drawing of a dog. If a greater degree of difficulty is desired, the RI closes his eyes and the dog leads him to the drawing.

Variations:

– The RI has a basket of primary colored balls, some larger and some smaller.

– The dog extracts a ball and gives it to him and the RI will now use two criteria – color and dimension – to select an object indicated by the IP, either by naming it directly or as a function of the color and size of the ball (larger or smaller). If the selection is correct, the RI uses the object on the dog.

– One of the RIs performs a mime to represent an action related to the dog.

– The others observe closely. The one who first guesses the action selects the object needed for that action and places it in the dog's basket. If the selected item is the correct one, the RI who did the mime uses it on the dog.

COMMANDS FOR THE DOG	MATERIALS
• Fetch	• Cards of colored objects
• Carry	• Dog-related objects
• Get it	• Illustration of dog
• Sit	• Basket
• Stay	• Colored balls

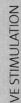

COGNITIVE STIMULATION

		Objectives
Psychomotor Area	Physical coordination	• Exercise visual perception: shape-form
	Sensory stimulation	• Improve oral comprehension
	Space-time perception	• Acquire or exercise notions of color and size
	Corporal awareness	• Recognize characteristics of objects
Cognitive Area	Atention and concentration	• Establish relationships between objects
	Recognition of categories	• Enrich vocabulary
	Memory	• Stimulate group communication
	Language and communication	• Enhance verbal expression
Social-emotional Area	Presentation	• Explore different means of communication
	Activity	
	Leave-taking and relaxation	
	Board games	

The objective is for the RI to "win" several objects and then do something with them.

We have three or more chairs, each one of which represents a shop or type of business: bakery, grocer, pharmacy, veterinary clinic, etc. Each "station" has products typical to it and is also distinguished by a card illustrating a particular canine trick or skill.

The dog will perform a trick or skill, and the RIs must associate it with the shop or business having that card. The first one to correctly identify the station goes there and, without the others seeing, selects an object or a card. His companions must now determine, by way of "yes or no" questions, what object or card the RI has selected.

When an RI correctly identifies the object, the operation is repeated until the round is completed. The RI can also decide which shop he wants to go to, but he must have the dog perform the trick or skill associated with that particular station. If the association is correct, he can go to that station and select an object.

When all, or a sufficient number, of the objects have been selected and identified, they can be put to use in, for example, drawing up a menu, setting a table, outfitting a veterinary clinic or a doctor's office.

Variations:

– We set out several chairs, each one corresponding to a part of the human face. On them we place models or drawings of different sized noses, various colors of eyes, shapes of mouths, fine or bushy eyebrows, big or small ears, different colored hair, etc. Each of the stations has a canine trick or skill associated with it. The RIs watch the dog perform a trick or skill in order to know to which station one must go to select that particular part of the face.

– The RIs then use these pieces to compose a face, which may well be a funny one. Then one of the RIs chooses a particular trick or skill, which in turn indicates to another RI which station to select a feature from. He puts the feature (nose, mouth, etc.) in its place on the outline of the face, then commands the dog to do another trick, and so on until the face is complete.

COMMANDS FOR THE DOG	MATERIALS
• Jump / Weave	• Skills cards
• Bang / Back	• Everyday objects / Fruits
• Roll over / Twist	• Cards illustrating everyday life

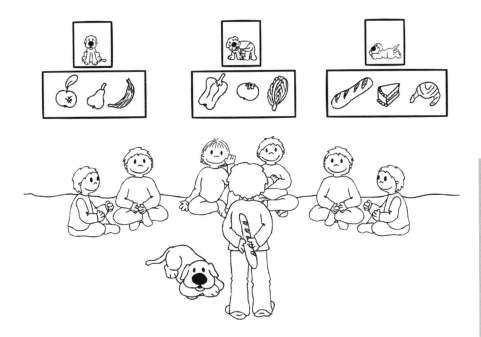

		Objectives
Psychomotor Area	Physical coordination	• Acquire or exercise the capacity to use symbols
	Sensory stimulation	• Acquire or exercise the capacity to concentrate
	Space-time perception	• Develop or evaluate short-term memory
	Corporal awareness	• Establish relationships between objects
Cognitive Area	Atention and concentration	• Recognize characteristics of objects
	Recognition of categories	• Stimulate creativity: diverse ways of thinking
	Memory	• Stimulate the imagination
	Language and communication	• Develop symbolic thinking
Social-emotional Area	Presentation	• Encourage socialization
	Activity	• Learn and respect social norms
	Leave-taking and relaxation	• Discover elements of adult social life
	Board games	

The objective of this activity is for the RI to resolve a problem posed by the IP.

The RI and the IP must jointly think through possible strategies for achieving the desired result.

The AIT makes sure the dog shows sustained interest in the reasoning put forth by the RI and encourages the animal to use its eyes and physical contact to contribute the search for a solution to the problem.

When the RI proposes an action, the dog, with help from the AIT, carries out that action as a way of seeing whether it helps achieve the objective. The AIT must take care in preventing the dog from resolving the problem too soon on its own.

We show the RI that even small steps toward a goal can be big strides on the way to a solution; moves that he must appreciate and encourage through clicking and treats.

1. Teach the dog to fetch an object in box
2. Teach the dog a trick
3. Prepare the dog's food, with variable degrees of complexity
4. Jump through a hoop covered with tissue paper
5. Making "baskets" with balls tossed into an appropriate-level receptacle or through a hoop
6. Picking up papers from the floor and throwing them in the wastebasket.

COMMANDS FOR THE DOG	MATERIALS
• Get it	• Box
• Sit	• Hoops
• Look	• Broad-width tissue paper
• Yes	• Clicker and treats
• No	

		Objectives
Psychomotor Area	Physical coordination	• Learn to appraise a problem realistically
	Sensory stimulation	• Search for possible and viable solutions
	Space-time perception	• Acquire or exercise the capacity to concentrate
	Corporal awareness	• Stimulate creativity and use of the imagination
Cognitive Area	Atention and concentration	• Learn and respect social norms
	Recognition of categories	• Exercise eye-body coordination
	Memory	• Experience the pleasure of achievement
	Language and communication	• Create affective bonds
Social-emotional Area	Presentation	• Learn to make decisions
	Activity	
	Leave-taking and relaxation	
	Board games	

psycho-motor activity exercises

psycho-motor

activity

exercises

The objective is for the RI to perform or simulate a series of grooming or recreational activities with the dog, combining them with psycho-motor exercises.

Most of the exercise takes place along a circuit. Before beginning, each team chooses a color that represents it. Upon completing the circuit, the RI affixes an adhesive label of his team's color to a mural.

Each turn or "lap" around the course begins with putting the collar and leash on the dog. Then we go through the following activities:

– Cross a "river" of hoops
– Put a handkerchief of the team's color around the dog's neck
– "Slalom" through cones
– Brush the dog
– Walk together between two lines
– Put food in a bowl and feed the dog
– Throw hoops to the dog
– Simulate picking up dog poop and throwing it in the garbage
– Go up and down a ramp
– Take the handkerchief off the dog

At the end, he takes a label of the team's color and affixes it to the mural.

COMMANDS FOR THE DOG	MATERIALS
• Sit	• Collar and leash
• Down	• Hoops
• Heel	• Colors die
	• Colored handkerchiefs
	• Feeding bowl
	• Chalk
	• Goad
	• Ramp

	Physical coordination	Objectives
Psychomotor Area	Sensory stimulation	• Learn and follow social norms
	Space-time perception	• Exercise gross motor skills
	Corporal awareness	• Exercise hand-eye coordination
Cognitive Area	Atention and concentration	• Develop accuracy and precision
	Recognition of categories	• Develop or evaluate short-term memory
	Memory	• Exercise sense of right-left
	Language and communication	• Acquire or exercise the ability to concentrate
Social-emotional Area	Presentation	
	Activity	
	Leave-taking and relaxation	
	Board games	

PSYCHO-MOTOR ACTIVITY

The objective is for the RI, together with the dog, to follow instructions from the therapist outside an area with defined boundaries.

The RI, with the dog on a leash, walks clockwise around the perimeter of a previously marked-off space.

The RI moves around the room using different kinds of locomotion (walking, running, jumping with legs together or apart, rolling, slithering, crawling, etc.) without touching the boundary of the area marked off with tape.

The RI must listen for the following directives from the IP:

– "Inside": The RI and the dog must enter the area, where they can move around in different ways but without touching the boundary line.

– "Outside": The RI and the dog must exit the area and move around, again respecting the line.

Variations:

– The RI gives the "inside" and "outside" commands to the dog. When they are both on the same side of the boundary, either inside or outside, the RI imitates a skill of the dog.

– We draw a circle on the floor with chalk. The IP explains the RI that every time he says "inside," the RI must enter the circle and every time he says "outside," he must exit it. Then the orders can be given separately to the dog and to the RI, who must distinguish when it is his turn and when it's not.

– We have the RI make the dog go into and come out of an animal travel crate, following commands from the IP or issuing the commands himself.

COMMANDS FOR THE DOG	MATERIALS
• Stay	• Chalk
• Stand	• Travel crate
• Get it	

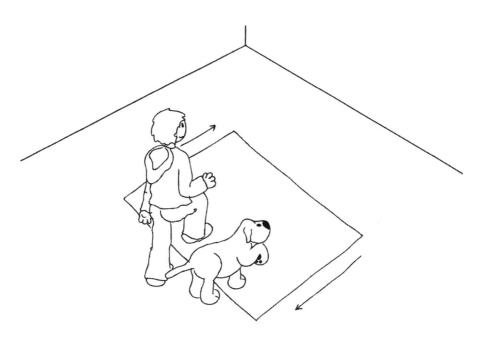

	Physical coordination	Objectives
Psychomotor Area	Sensory stimulation	• Exercise gross motor skills
	Space-time perception	• Exercise sense of place in space
	Corporal awareness	• Pay attention to instructions
Cognitive Area	Atention and concentration	• Pay attention to the movements of others
	Recognition of categories	• Acquire or exercise ability to concentrate
	Memory	• Improve oral comprehension
	Language and communication	• Learn and respect social norms
Social-emotional Area	Presentation	• Stimulate active listening
	Activity	
	Leave-taking and relaxation	
	Board games	

PSYCHO-MOTOR ACTIVITY

259

FOUR DIRECTIONS

The objective of this game is for the RI to put into practice the spatial concepts of "in front of" and "behind," as well as those of "right" and "left."

We place five hoops on the floor, one in the center and the other four forming a cross.

The RI takes his place at the center of the cross, with both feet inside the hoop. The IP or the dog indicates to the RI where they want him to go by showing him cards.

If it is the dog,

— he takes the RI a card in his mouth or in a basket
— he touches his snout to a card on the wall
— his sits on a certain card.

The RI follows the instruction moving only one foot, leaving the other in the central hop. The dog determines whether the movement is correct or not.

If the dog passes between the RI's legs, the movement was correct. If he sits down before passing through, the movement was incorrect.

Variations:

— We can make two crosses, one for the RI and the other for the dog. The two must follow the IP's directions simultaneously.

COMMANDS FOR THE DOG	MATERIALS
• Get it	• Five hoops
• Mark	• "In Front-Behind" card
• Sit	• "Left-Right" card
• Stay	• Spatial directions die

		Objectives
Psychomotor Area	Physical coordination	• Exercise gross motor skills
	Sensory stimulation	• Exercise balance
	Space-time perception	• Control bodily movement
	Corporal awareness	• Acquire or exercise notion of space and direction
Cognitive Area	Atention and concentration	• Acquire or exercise ability to concentrate
	Recognition of categories	• Improve oral comprehension
	Memory	• Learn and respect social norms
	Language and communication	
Social-emotional Area	Presentation	
	Activity	
	Leave-taking and relaxation	
	Board games	

261

STOP, COME

The objective of this game is for the RI to follow, in the street, directions from the IP.

They go out to the street to take a walk. They arrange themselves on the sidewalk with the therapist closest to the street, then the RI, then the dog, then another IP, closest to the buildings. This disposition assures the safety of the RI during the walk.

— Upon hearing the command "Stop," the RI and the dog immediately halt. If the RI obeys this instruction, he gets to give the dog a treat. This is repeated several times. When the RI is consistently obeying the directive, the following commands will be given at random:

— "Let's go": The RI gives the command to the dog to resume the walk

— "Come" (for the RI): The therapist moves a certain distance away with a treat in his hand. He makes eye contact with the RI and instructs him to come, either verbally or by way of a hand signal. The RI approaches him with the dog and the IP gives the RI the treat to give to the dog.

— "Come" (for the dog): We place the treat on the ground a certain distance from the dog. To encourage the RI to give the command, we tell him to go pick up the treat and call the dog to come to him. The dog is waiting calmly in the "sit" position. When the RI calls him, he goes to him to receive the treat.

COMMANDS FOR THE DOG	MATERIALS
• Stop	• Treats
• Let's go	
• Come	
• Treat	

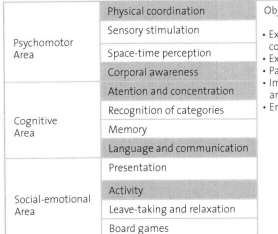

		Objectives
Psychomotor Area	Physical coordination	
	Sensory stimulation	• Exercise overall dynamic coordination
	Space-time perception	• Exercise body-sight coordination
	Corporal awareness	• Pay attention to instructions
Cognitive Area	Atention and concentration	• Improve language comprehension and expression
	Recognition of categories	• Enhance self-esteem
	Memory	
	Language and communication	
Social-emotional Area	Presentation	
	Activity	
	Leave-taking and relaxation	
	Board games	

The objective is for the RI to distinguish between two shapes or two colors.

We lay out a circuit with cones and mushrooms of the same color, or with either only cones or only mushrooms of two different colors.

The IP and the dog navigate the course demonstrating what the RI will do, such as using the command "sit" to have the dog sit each time a mushroom is reached.

As we continue with this exercise, we teach the RI different ways to command the dog to sit.

– Standing at the dog's side and touching his rump
– Touch the rump and say the command
– Standing in front of the dog, show him a fist
– Show the fist and say the command

We can lay out the circuit in a straight line or in a circle, adjusting its difficulty to the capabilities of the RI. For example:

– Alternate cones and mushrooms, where the dog must sit, in a straight line
– Alternate the "sits" at the mushrooms with other actions to be performed at the cones: touch, pet, kiss, brush or give a treat to the dog.
– Alternate mushroom-"sit", cones-actions and various obstacles.

Variations:

– Introduce the command for another trick or skill at the mushrooms. The command can be chosen by the IP, the dog, by use of the dice, cards or a wheel, or the RI can indicate by word or gesture what he wants the dog to do.

COMMANDS FOR THE DOG	MATERIALS
• Sit	• Mushrooms
• Various tricks and skills	• Cones
• Heel	• Cards
• Stand	• Colors die
	• Skills die
	• Objects for laying out circuit

	Physical coordination	Objectives
Psychomotor Area	Sensory stimulation	• Acquire or exercise notion of colors
	Space-time perception	• Acquire or exercise notion of geometric shapes
	Corporal awareness	• Exercise sense of place in space
Cognitive Area	Atention and concentration	• Develop concentration • Pay attention to movements of others
	Recognition of categories	
	Memory	• Develop symbolic thinking: codification and de-codification of symbols
	Language and communication	
Social-emotional Area	Presentation	• Stimulate group action and communication
	Activity	
	Leave-taking and relaxation	
	Board games	

The objective is for the RI to imitate the dog's movements and to engage in a pleasurable activity with him.

We use chalk to draw a path, not too wide, around the dog.

The RI then must follow the path, moving with the mode of locomotion indicated by the dog.

The dog will show with his own movements whether the RI should progress walking on all fours, with his hands raised, slithering like a snake, rolling, walking backwards, sitting on his rear, etc.

Each time the IP claps, the dog adopts a new posture and the RI changes his manner of moving along the path.

Variations:

– The RI spins the animals wheel on which are indicated various methods of locomotion. The challenge is for both the dog and the RI to imitate the animal and move in a way that resembles as closely as possible the way the animal moves. If it is impossible for the dog to imitate the animal that came up, the dog accompanies the RI by performing a skill and may receive a treat from him.

COMMANDS FOR THE DOG	MATERIALS
• Shame	• Chalk
• Up	• Animals wheel
• Back	• Skills wheel
• Crawl	
• Jump	
• Roll over	
• Beg	
• Stand	
• Down	
• Sit	
• Twist	

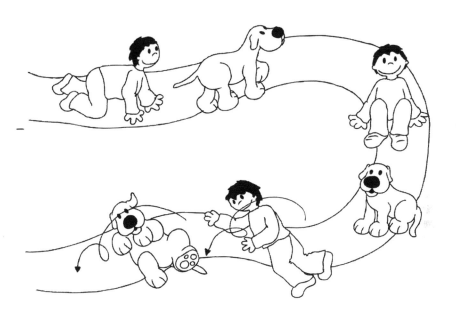

		Objectives
Psychomotor Area	Physical coordination	• Exercise overall dynamic coordination
	Sensory stimulation	• Exercise balance
	Space-time perception	• Develop a mental picture of body structure and anatomy
	Corporal awareness	• Exercise sense of rhythm
Cognitive Area	Atention and concentration	• Pay attention to movements of others
	Recognition of categories	• Acquire or exercise the ability to imitate
	Memory	• Develop symbolic thinking
	Language and communication	• Stimulate the imagination
Social-emotional Area	Presentation	• Experience the pleasure of movement
	Activity	• Experience the pleasure of laughter
	Leave-taking and relaxation	
	Board games	

267

COLORED FRISBEES

The objective of this game is for the RI to throw a Frisbee to the dog.

We set out some colored cones with a certain distance between them. In another part of the field sits a basket full of colored Frisbees.

The RI and the dog go together to the basket and the RI chooses a Frisbee. They then proceed to the matching color cone.

If the RI has matched the colors correctly, he gets to throw the Frisbee to the dog, who returns it to him for a treat.

Variations:

– The RI can match up various objects in pairs. When he does it correctly, he gets to throw the Frisbee to the dog.

– Draw numbers from one basket and cards indicating mathematical operations from another. Do the operation with the chosen numbers. If the RI gets the right answer, he throws the Frisbee to the dog.

– Match up cards showing dog grooming objects with the real tools.

– Match up opposites.

COMMANDS FOR THE DOG	MATERIALS
• Carry • Fetch • Heel	• Colored cones • Colored Frisbees • Baskets • Cards with numbers and mathematical operations • Objects for matching

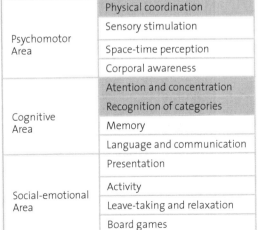

	Physical coordination	Objectives
Psychomotor Area	Sensory stimulation	• Exercise gross motor skills
	Space-time perception	• Acquire or exercise notion of geometric shapes
	Corporal awareness	• Acquire or exercise notion of sizes
Cognitive Area	Atention and concentration	• Acquire or exercise notion of numbers and quantity
	Recognition of categories	• Acquire or exercise notion of colors
	Memory	
	Language and communication	
Social-emotional Area	Presentation	
	Activity	
	Leave-taking and relaxation	
	Board games	

269

The objective of this game is for the RI to follow the dog and imitate his movements.

We lay out a circuit with various obstacles around the room or the yard.

The IP and the dog complete a demonstration round of the circuit, with the IP urging the RIs to closely observe the dog's movements.

Depending on the willingness of the dog, we can use different methods for following him:

– Holding onto his tail
– Put a belt around his waist
– Follow without physical contact

The RIs will have to negotiate several obstacles:

– Go up and down a ramp
– Jump over a bar
– Go over a bench
– Go under a bar
– Go through a tunnel

To make it more fun, the dog can perform tricks such as twist, up, beg, roll over, etc. between the obstacles.

Variations:

– Each RI, by way of questions or actions, gets a colored handkerchief. The IP says a color and the RI with that color handkerchief uses it to "hook up" to the dog or to a companion, forming a train that follows the dog.

– This game can be played to music. When the music stops, the train stops, too.

COMMANDS FOR THE DOG	MATERIALS
• Get it	• Tunnel
• Skills or tricks with gesture commands	• Bars
	• Cones
	• Benches
	• Chests
	• Handkerchiefs
	• Colors wheel
	• Music
	• Leashes

	Physical coordination	Objectives
Psychomotor Area	Sensory stimulation	• Exercise overall global coordination
	Space-time perception	• Exercise gross motor skills • Exercise sense of place in space
	Corporal awareness	• Exercise sense of place in time • Exercise balance
Cognitive Area	Atention and concentration	• Exercise sense of right-left • Develop image of body structure:
	Recognition of categories	mental image of imitated person's
	Memory	movements
	Language and communication	• Pay attention to movements of others
Social-emotional Area	Presentation	• Acquire or exercise ability to concentrate
	Activity	• Develop or evaluate short-term memory
	Leave-taking and relaxation	• Learn and respect social norms
	Board games	

271

The objective of this game is for the participants to pass a ball among themselves.

The players take their places in a circle or one in front of the other. Before tossing the ball, the RI must call out the name of the person to whom he wants to pass it in order for the recipient to be ready.

The game begins with a certain number of balls. If a ball falls to the floor (is not caught), the dog gets a point. He retrieves the fallen ball and takes it to his basket.

At the end of the game, we count the balls the dog has and those the RIs have. If the dog has more, he indicates to the RIs that he wants them to perform some psycho-motor exercises. If the RIs have more balls, they get to command the dog to perform some tricks or skills.

Variations:

– We divide the players into two teams and form two lines with enough space to toss a ball between the teammates. When the dog rings a bell with its paw, the last person in line on each team tosses the ball to the teammate ahead of him.

Each player tosses the ball to the next until it reaches the player at the head of the line. He tosses the ball to his team's dog, who catches it in his mouth and takes it to his team's basket. The first team to get all the balls into its basket wins.

The dog can also "make a basket" by tossing the ball into his team's basket instead of just depositing it there.

COMMANDS FOR THE DOG	MATERIALS
• Stand	• Colored balls
• Carry	• Baskets
• Catch	• Cards illustrating tricks and skills
• Basket	• Bell
• Various tricks	• Skills die
• Shoot basket	

		Objectives
Psychomotor Area	Physical coordination	• Exercise gross motor skills
	Sensory stimulation	• Exercise hand-eye coordination
	Space-time perception	• Develop aim and accuracy
	Corporal awareness	• Moderate volume of voice
Cognitive Area	Atention and concentration	• Pay attention to instructions
	Recognition of categories	• Acquire notions of arithmetic: addition and subtraction
	Memory	• Develop social interaction
	Language and communication	• Stimulate communication and interaction within group
Social-emotional Area	Presentation	• Introducing oneself
	Activity	• Accept norms of social interaction
	Leave-taking and relaxation	• Stimulate communication between groups
	Board games	• Enhance relationships of affinity

THE DOG'S TRUNK

The objective of this game is for the RI to explain to the dog how to play with the toys in his trunk.

The IP places several objects he wants the RI to work with into a trunk, saying they are the dog's toys.

The RI takes an object from the trunk with the dog at his side. If the exercise is designed to aid in regaining physical ability, the box can be placed at various heights or distances to create the appropriate degree of difficulty.

The RI describes the object he has chosen, with or without help from the therapist, then tosses it to the dog.

The dog returns the object to the RI, who explains in detail the properties of the toy while to dog looks at him or leans against him.

Variations:

– We put objects that are emotionally relevant to the RI in the trunk. He takes them out one at a time and, with or without the help of the therapist, tells the dog his thoughts and feelings about each one.

– We put personal hygiene and grooming items in the trunk, so the RI can explain to the dog what they are for and how they are used.

– The RI, using only his sense of touch, must guess which object he has grabbed in the trunk. If he's right, he can toss it to the dog.

– We ask the RI to list by memory the object he has withdrawn from the trunk.

COMMANDS FOR THE DOG	MATERIALS
• Sit	• Trunk
• Bring	• Objects to work with
• Give	
• Look	
• Head down	

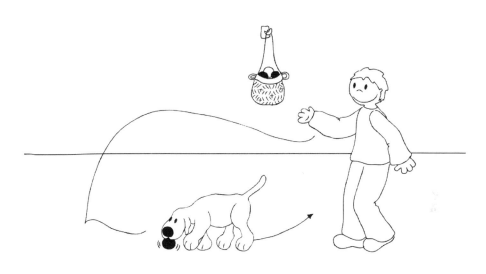

	Physical coordination	Objectives
Psychomotor Area	Sensory stimulation	• Exercise fine motor skills
	Space-time perception	• Exercise sense of touch
	Corporal awareness	• Exercise observation of movement of objects through space
Cognitive Area	Atention and concentration	• Moderate volume of voice
	Recognition of categories	• Accept norms of social interaction
	Memory	• Establish relationships between objects
	Language and communication	• Develop language comprehension and expression
Social-emotional Area	Presentation	• Enrich vocabulary
	Activity	• Lengthen attention span
	Leave-taking and relaxation	• Work on elements of daily routine
	Board games	• Develop or evaluate long-term memory

PSYCHO-MOTOR ACTIVITY

The objective of the game is to complete an obstacle course and earn pieces of a puzzle forming the image of a dog.

The course comprises obstacles made of inanimate objects and obstacles formed by the dog himself, with the canine challenges coming immediately after each physical barrier.

The RI must:

– jump over a bar
– step over a bench
– toss hoops over a peg or over the dog's head
– go under a bar, etc.

The dog takes up a position immediately after each obstacle, where the RI must complete an action with him:

– step over the prostrate dog
– go around the dog either jumping, walking or running
– make a figure 8 with two dogs
– pass beneath the dog

Upon completing the circuit, the IP gives a puzzle piece to the RI, who must identify the part of the dog's body it represents. He can either touch that part on the dog or affix an adhesive label there.

The RIs then gather around a table and put together the dog puzzle using the pieces they earned by completing the obstacle course.

Variations:

– Upon completing his turn on the course, the RI tosses the body parts die and must locate and take the corresponding puzzle piece.

COMMANDS FOR THE DOG	MATERIALS
• Down • Stand	• Bars and cones • Benches or steps • Hoops • Puzzle pieces • Body parts die

	Physical coordination	Objectives
Psychomotor Area	Sensory stimulation	• Exercise gross motor skills
	Space-time perception	• Promote symmetrical movement • Promote asymmetrical movement
	Corporal awareness	• Exercise inhibition of movement
Cognitive Area	Atention and concentration	• Exercise balance • Acquire or exercise ability to
	Recognition of categories	concentrate
	Memory	• Improve language comprehension and expression
	Language and communication	• Accept norms of social interaction
Social-emotional Area	Presentation	
	Activity	
	Leave-taking and relaxation	
	Board games	

277

DOG TWISTER

The objective of this game is for the participants in the session to work their bodies into complicated positions that the dog will try to pass through.

We have a mat with circles of different colors, or we can use different colored hoops arrayed on the floor. We adjust the difficulty of the game to the capabilities of the participating RIs.

The dog brings a ball in his mouth or in a basket and one of the RIs looks at it. Another participant spins the body parts wheel or throws the body parts die, who retrieves it. The players on the mat must put the body part that came up on a circle of the same color as the ball.

When all the players on the mat are "positioned," the dog tries to find his way through them.

Variations:

– If there are few players, it can be the IP who says which body part must go on which color.

COMMANDS FOR THE DOG	MATERIALS
• Get it • Crawl	• Mat with colored circles • Colored hoops • Colored balls • Body parts wheel • Body parts die

		Objectives
Psychomotor Area	Physical coordination	• Exercise gross motor skills
	Sensory stimulation	• Exercise balance
	Space-time perception	• Develop mental image of body structure
	Corporal awareness	• Acquire or exercise notion of colors
Cognitive Area	Atention and concentration	• Improve language comprehension and expression
	Recognition of categories	• Stimulate group communication and interaction
	Memory	• Experience the pleasure of laughter
	Language and communication	• Learn to await one's turn
Social-emotional Area	Presentation	
	Activity	
	Leave-taking and relaxation	
	Board games	

The objective of this game is to memorize an activity and repeat it backward, in other words, in other words retell beginning from the end.

We lay out a circuit the difficulty of which is determined by the capabilities of each RI. After completing it a couple of times, we ask the RI that he do it again only this time beginning at the finish line and going toward the starting line.

These could be some of the obstacles

- Pass over a roller with his legs apart and the dog at his side
- Go around a table and give a treat to the dog
- Have the dog jump up on a chair and pet his head
- Jump over a roller or a bar and have the dog jump, too

To emphasize and make visibly concrete the idea of doing and undoing, we can add this element to the exercise: going forward on the circuit, each time the RI successfully negotiates an obstacle, the IP puts an item of clothing on the dog. At the finish line, the dog is dressed.

When the RI does the circuit backward, each time he successfully negotiates an obstacle, either he or the IP removes a piece of the dog's clothing. When original starting line is reached, the dog is undressed.

Variations:

− On the forward lap, each time the IP puts a piece of clothing on the dog, the RI sits next to the animal. The IP asks him to recall a pleasant feeling or experience and describe it. On the "backward" lap, each time the IP removes an article of clothing, the RI relates an unpleasant experience or feeling.

COMMANDS FOR THE DOG	MATERIALS
• Heel	• Roller or tube
• Treat	• Bar and cones
• Up	• Four items of clothing modified
• Jump	for the dog

	Physical coordination	Objectives
Psychomotor Area	Sensory stimulation	• Develop or evaluate visual memory
	Space-time perception	• Acquire or exercise ability to concentrate
	Corporal awareness	• Exercise gross motor skills
Cognitive Area	Atention and concentration	• Exercise fine motor skills
	Recognition of categories	• Learn to codify and de-codify
	Memory	• Enhance self-esteem
	Language and communication	• Express feelings: sadness, happiness, anger
Social-emotional Area	Presentation	
	Activity	
	Leave-taking and relaxation	
	Board games	

PSYCHO-MOTOR ACTIVITY

The objective of this game is for the RIs to pass a plastic egg along to each other, each one saying the name of the person next to them before passing it on.

We have the players form a line or semicircle. The IP stands in front of them with the dog at his side in the "stay" position.

The IP tosses the body parts die to determine with which part of the body the players will hold the egg: under the chin, in the hand, between the knees, in the armpit, in the bend of the elbow, etc.

The RIs will pass the egg in this manner until the dog changes position or makes a move different from that made at the toss of the die, for example: if he was sitting, he stands; if he was twisting, he'll play dead. When that happens, the game immediately stops and the person holding the egg must step forward and imitate the movement the dog was making right before the change. The IP then tosses the die again to resume the game.

Variations:

– With one or several RIs, we can decide a sequence of skills the dog must perform. The players pass the egg and when the IP claps his hands, the person with the egg must tell the dog the trick or skill he must do.

COMMANDS FOR THE DOG	MATERIALS
• Sit	• Plastic egg
• Stay	• Skills cards
• Various tricks and skills	• Body parts die

		Objectives
Psychomotor Area	Physical coordination	• Exercise overall dynamic coordination • Develop mental image of body structure • Imitate movements: body control • Pay attention to instructions • Pay attention to movements of others • Acquire or exercise ability to imitate • Learn names • Stimulate communication within group
	Sensory stimulation	
	Space-time perception	
	Corporal awareness	
Cognitive Area	Atention and concentration	
	Recognition of categories	
	Memory	
	Language and communication	
Social-emotional Area	Presentation	
	Activity	
	Leave-taking and relaxation	
	Board games	

The objective is for the RI to throw various objects in an effort to hit the dog bone.

In order to foster control and accuracy in throwing objects over varying distances, we place a dog bone on the floor and ask the RI to toss some balls and try to hit it.

Every time the ball touches the bone, the dog will do a trick. When the RI misses, he must perform a certain action.

The therapist decides how far away to place the bone, taking into account the size, weight and texture of the ball to be thrown.

Variations:

– Tossing hoops over the dog's head. We ask the RI to take aim and toss a hoop over the dog's head so it lands on his neck. The dog is seated and still at a certain distance. The AIT makes sure the dog won't be struck in a way that will hurt, placing the animal at a distance he feels confident the RI can manage successfully.

– The RI must recognize a canine skill card shown to him by the IP and, employing the right tone of voice and gesture, give the dog the correct command to perform that trick or skill. If the dog performs the skill, the RI can throw him a ball in a game of "catch."

COMMANDS FOR THE DOG	MATERIALS
• Various tricks: twist, up, bang, back, cross, roll over....	• Dog bones • Balls • Skills die • Deck of skills cards

	Physical coordination	Objectives
Psychomotor Area	Sensory stimulation	• Exercise hand-eye coordination
	Space-time perception	• Exercise visual perception: background-figure
	Corporal awareness	• Exercise tactile perception
Cognitive Area	Atention and concentration	• Develop muscle-control and strength
	Recognition of categories	• Develop aim and accuracy
	Memory	• Accept norms of social interaction
	Language and communication	• Experience the pleasure of achievement
Social-emotional Area	Presentation	• Experience the pleasure of laughter
	Activity	
	Leave-taking and relaxation	
	Board games	

PSYCHO-MOTOR ACTIVITY

The objective of this game is for the RI to learn and recognize the parts of the dog's body or the dog's emotions so as to be able to relate them to human anatomy and feelings.

We hang on the wall a large photo of a dog similar to the therapy dog, or we place a good-sized stuffed-animal (plush) dog on a table. The RI throws balls painted with finger paints at different parts of the body of the dog in the photograph, or balls with Velcro at the stuffed-animal dog.

Each time he hits the target, he must recognize the body part, name it, touch it on the therapy dog and touch it on himself. We can also ask him to explain the main function of that body part.

Variation using dog emotions:

– We attach oversize cards to the wall showing human faces expressing different emotions.

The dog takes to the RI cards illustrating various canine emotional states. Upon receiving each such card, the RI and the AIT try to identify the dog's feelings or state of mind and discuss what kind of situation might have prompted that emotion in the animal.

Then the RI tries to identify that emotion in the pictures of the human faces, and throws a ball at that image.

If the selection is correct, he tells the therapist what kind of situation or circumstances produce that emotion in him. Then he throws the ball for the dog to fetch.

COMMANDS FOR THE DOG	MATERIALS
• Fetch	• Large illustration or photo of dog
• Give	• Velcro balls
• Carry	• Images of facial expressions
• Stand	

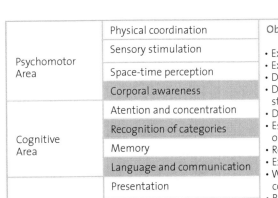

		Objectives
Psychomotor Area	Physical coordination	• Exercise fine motor skills
	Sensory stimulation	• Exercise hand-eye coordination
	Space-time perception	• Develop idea of body structure
	Corporal awareness	• Develop muscle-control and strength
Cognitive Area	Atention and concentration	• Develop aim and accuracy
	Recognition of categories	• Establish r.elationships between objects
	Memory	• Recognize characteristics of objects
	Language and communication	• Express feelings
Social-emotional Area	Presentation	• Work with non-verbal communication
	Activity	• Recognize others' expressions of emotion
	Leave-taking and relaxation	
	Board games	

The objective of this activity is for the RI to imitate a posture adopted by the dog in order to receive the appreciation and positive reinforcement of his companions.

We proceed according to the premise of positive training: "Let's make a deal:

Every time you do something well, I will acknowledge that with a click and then I'll give you a treat." We do this exercise so that both the RI and the dog receive their own rewards.

We make two stacks of cards: one with dog tricks and the other with postures of human/canine yoga. These images, created with digital special effects, can be seen in a poster titled, "Canine Yoga."

To begin, RI1 asks one of his companions, RI2, to activate the clicker immediately after the dog performs a certain trick. Then RI1 gives the dog a reward – either a caress or a dog treat.

Now RI2 selects a card from the human/canine yoga deck. He observes it closely, then passes it to another participant, RI3, who, once RI2 has assumed the illustrated position, applauds him and pays him a compliment.

We continue playing until all present have had the dog perform a trick and assumed a yoga position.

Variations:

– The dog performs a trick and the RI clicks and rewards him. Then the RI imitates the postion adopted by the dog and the IP applauds and congratulates him.

COMMANDS FOR THE DOG	MATERIALS
• Various tricks and skills	• Dog skills cards
	• Yoga positions cards
	• Cards of canine yoga

		Objectives
Psychomotor Area	Physical coordination	• Exercise overall dynamic coordination
	Sensory stimulation	• Exercise balance and sense of left-right
	Space-time perception	• Develop idea of body structure
	Corporal awareness	• Pay attention to movements of others
Cognitive Area	Atention and concentration	• Acquire or exercise the ability to imitate
	Recognition of categories	• Develop powers of observation and visual memory
	Memory	• Develop social interaction
	Language and communication	• Develop sociable behaviors
Social-emotional Area	Presentation	• Develop the ability to relate to others' emotions
	Activity	
	Leave-taking and relaxation	
	Board games	

CLOSING YOUR CLOTHES

The objective of this activity is for the RI to learn to use and manipulate different mechanisms for closing items of clothing (zippers, buttons, Velcro, etc.) as well as means of closing other objects such as jars and containers.

1 - With jars and purses of treats: We place along a circuit an array of jars and purses containing treats. The key element here is that each the jars or purses is closed with a different type of mechanism that the RI must manipulate and open in order to take out the treat and give it to the dog.

As the RI proceeds along the circuit and does different things, he finds the jars and purses. At each one, he sits and opens it, takes out the treat and gives it to the dog.

Variations:

– Give him a large doll with pockets having different kinds of closures and hide the treats inside them.

2- With CTAC leashes: We suggest that the RI take the dog for a walk. When he opens the box with the leashes, he finds them in pieces. He must reconstruct a leash using the different means of closure provided, then put it on the dog to go out for a walk.

Variations:

– We place the pieces of leash on the floor and ask the RI to identify on his own clothing the different types of closing mechanism found on the leash pieces. Then the AIT distributes the lengths of leash at random among all the RIs. Each RI must find the companion with the piece of leash that can be connected to his own. Working together, they reconstruct all the leashes, then take the dogs for a walk.

– The dog takes a picture of a certain closure mechanism to the RI. He looks among the leashes and finds the one with that type of closure and attaches it to the dog's collar.

COMMANDS FOR THE DOG	MATERIALS
• Heel	• CTAC leashes
• Treat	• Jars with different closing
• Get it	mechanisms
• Speak	
• Stay	

		Objectives
Psychomotor Area	Physical coordination	• Exercise fine motor skills • Exercise hand-eye coordination • Experience the pleasure of achievement • Experience the pleasure of effectively handling an object • Develop self-motivation • Increase tolerance of frustration
	Sensory stimulation	
	Space-time perception	
	Corporal awareness	
Cognitive Area	Atention and concentration	
	Recognition of categories	
	Memory	
	Language and communication	
Social-emotional Area	Presentation	
	Activity	
	Leave-taking and relaxation	
	Board games	

DOG COLLAGE

The objective of this activity is to make a collage representing a dog.

We place around the room several boxes with materials for making a collage. They can be hidden beneath cones or set on objects of varying height.

The RI walks the dog around the room and picks up the materials he finds.

When he finishes this "search," he can make his collage on a template. He can use, among other things: dog fur, cotton, ground dry dog food, small pieces of dog food, sawdust, woll, glue, etc.

In the course of doing this, the RI manipulates several types of material, and ends up with a souvenir from the session on which we write his name and that of the therapy dog.

Variations:

– Find the collage materials in jars whose contents are of varying textures.

– Role-playing of buying and selling. Taking part are the RI, the dog, the IP or another RI, working on social skills, verbal and non-verbal communication.

COMMANDS FOR THE DOG	MATERIALS
• Stay	• Collage materials: fur, dog food,
• Speak	cotton, fabric, etc.
• Down	• Template with image of a dog
• Beg	• Jars with different materials:
• Paw	rice, lentils, water, dog food, etc.
• Get it	
• Heel	
• Treat	

	Physical coordination	Objectives
Psychomotor Area	Sensory stimulation	• Exercise fine motor skills
	Space-time perception	• Exercise hand-eye coordination
	Corporal awareness	• Exercise spatial orientation
Cognitive Area	Atention and concentration	• Stimulate group communication and interaction
	Recognition of categories	• Learn and respect social norms
	Memory	• Discover elements of adult social life
	Language and communication	• Diminish shyness and withdrawal
Social-emotional Area	Presentation	• Verbal and non-verbal communication
	Activity	
	Leave-taking and relaxation	
	Board games	

PSYCHO-MOTOR ACTIVITY

293

The objective of this game is for the RI and the dog to build a bowling alley.

In order to earn the different-colored pins or skittles, the RI must match up physical symptoms (described in the first person) with cards or drawings indicating feelings or emotions brought to him by the dog.

For example:

- I have a knot in my stomach, and can't stay still: I'm nervous.
- I feel like crying, and my brow is knitted: I'm sad
- I want to break something and my fists are clenched: I'm angry
- I feel like I'm floating and have a smile on my face: I'm happy
- I want to hide and my shoulders are hunched: I'm ashamed
- My heart is beating fast and hard and my eyes are open wide: I'm scared
- Everything bothers me and my face is red: I'm in a bad mood
- My body is weighing me down and I'm leaning on whatever is at hand: I'm tired

With every couplet formed, the RI earns a pin, which he places in the appropriate spot. When enough pins are set, the dog brings him the ball he can now use to roll down the alley and knock the pins over.

COMMANDS FOR THE DOG	MATERIALS
• Stay	• Ball
• Give	• Pins or skittles
• Carry	• Emotions cards

	Physical coordination	Objectives
Psychomotor Area	Sensory stimulation	• Exercise sight-body coordination
	Space-time perception	• Develop aim and accuracy
	Corporal awareness	• Develop symbolic thinking: codification and de-codification of symbols
Cognitive Area	Atention and concentration	• Improve verbal comprehension and expression
	Recognition of categories	• Stimulate group communication and interaction
	Memory	• Express personality
	Language and communication	• Manage feelings and emotions
Social-emotional Area	Presentation	• Express feelings: sadness, happiness, anger
	Activity	
	Leave-taking and relaxation	
	Board games	

PSYCHO-MOTOR ACTIVITY

295

The objective of this game is for the RI to find the mate of each of the single socks brought to him by the dog.

We have several pairs of socks. The IP, depending on the RI or the group he's working with, determines the degree of similarity among the pairs. We divide the socks into two piles, one from each pair going into each pile. One bunch is put into an open suitcase.

A sock from the other bunch is given to the dog.

The RI calls the dog, who moves toward him exhibiting the sock dangling from his mouth. The animal can take it directly to the RI or stop a few steps away, depending on the degree of difficulty we want to impose on the game.

Now the RI goes to the suitcase and must find in it that sock's mate before the dog finishes performing a certain action or completing a pre-determined circuit.

After forming several pairs, the RI chooses which ones he wants to put on the dog. The dog lies down belly-up and lets the RI put the socks on him while identifying the limb; "front left, front right, rear left," etc.

The nails on the front feet and the dew claw can make putting the socks on difficult, so the AIT should help the RI do this part of the activity. One sock from a pair is put on each foot, with the other from that pair being looped and knotted around the top of the placed one to keep it from sagging.

Variations:

– Put a treat in each sock. The RI must take it out in order to give it to the dog.

COMMANDS FOR THE DOG	MATERIALS
• Carry	• Socks
• Stand	• Suitcase
• Down	
• Belly	
• Stay	

		Objectives
Psychomotor Area	Physical coordination	• Exercise fine motor skills • Exercise sense of right-left • Acquire or exercise the notion of numbers and quantity • Acquire or exercise the notion of colors • Acquire or exercise the notion of size • Acquire or exercise the notion of geometric shapes • Develop or evaluate visual memory • Establish relationships between objects • Foster tactile recognition • Experience the pleasure of achievement • Improve decision-making ability
	Sensory stimulation	
	Space-time perception	
	Corporal awareness	
Cognitive Area	Atention and concentration	
	Recognition of categories	
	Memory	
	Language and communication	
Social-emotional Area	Presentation	
	Activity	
	Leave-taking and relaxation	
	Board games	

FROM 1 TO 10

The objective of this activity is for the RI to answer a series of questions to arrive at the "finish line," which is the number 10.

We draw ten boxes on the floor with chalk, laying them out according to the desired degree of difficulty: in a line, as a semi-circle or on a hopscotch-like grid. We number the boxes 1 through 10, with each one corresponding to a question.

1 Who am I and what am I like?
2 Who takes care of me and is concerned about me?
3 I feel proud when...
4 A pleasant memory
5 An unpleasant memory
6 What I like the most is...
7 My favorite TV show is...
8 My best friend (boy)
9 My best friend (girl)
10 What makes me most happy is...

The dog moves around the boxes to indicate in which of them the RI must toss the beanbag. If he succeeds in landing it in the box, he answers the corresponding question. If not, the turn passes to the other player, who has different-colored beanbag.

The game continues by turns, with the winner being the first to reach the number 10.

To keep the other participants in the session interested in the game, the IP asks those observing the contest about the answers given by the two players.

COMMANDS FOR THE DOG	MATERIALS
• Mark it (the numbers) • Carry (question card) • Give • Stand • Get it 	• Different colored beanbags • Hoops • Cards with questions

298

	Physical coordination	Objectives
Psychomotor Area	Sensory stimulation	• Develop the capacity to get to know others
	Space-time perception	• Diminish shyness and withdrawal
	Corporal awareness	• Become aware of one's own capabilities and limitations
Cognitive Area	Atention and concentration	• Foster self-knowledge
	Recognition of categories	• Develop a positive and accurate self-image
	Memory	• Foster positive group dynamic
	Language and communication	• Manage emotions and feelings
Social-emotional Area	Presentation	• Develop aim and accuracy
	Activity	• Learn to listen and respond
	Leave-taking and relaxation	• Accept norms for social interaction
	Board games	

PSYCHO-MOTOR ACTIVITY

The objective of this exercise is for the RI to follow written directions given to him by the dog.

The IP writes instructions on plastic-coated cards – so the dog can carry them in his mouth – or on pieces of paper if we want to place them in the CTAC dog blanket pockets or hide them somewhere in the room.

The directions will progress from uncomplicated to increasingly difficult. We can give instructions involving time and movement, regarding social or affective skills or having to do with parts of the body, among other things.

The RI obtains a card either by taking it from the dog blanket pocket, asking the dog to bring him one, earning it by way of performing a psycho-motor action (toss a ball, jump, etc.), having the dog do a trick, and so forth.

Upon obtaining the card, he attentively reads, or listens to, the instructions and performs the action with or without the help of an adult.

Variations:

– The RI reads or listens to a directive, the correctly relays it to a companion for him to carry out.

COMMANDS FOR THE DOG	MATERIALS
• Carry	• CTAC dog blanket
• Stay	
• Get it	
• Treat	
• Look	
• Stand	

	Physical coordination	Objectives
Psychomotor Area	Sensory stimulation	• Pay attention to instructions
	Space-time perception	• Acquire or exercise ability to concentrate
	Corporal awareness	• Develop symbolic thinking
Cognitive Area	Atention and concentration	• Learn and respect social norms
	Recognition of categories	• Learn to listen without interrupting
	Memory	• Reading
	Language and communication	• Improve language comprehension and expression
Social-emotional Area	Presentation	• Stimulate group communication and interaction
	Activity	• Develop ability to enjoy positive feelings
	Leave-taking and relaxation	
	Board games	

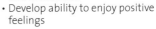

PSYCHO-MOTOR ACTIVITY

301

With this exercise we are encouraging the RI to get closer to the dog by way of delivering treats. Even if it's true that treat-giving becomes one of the things the RI will like most about his relationship with the dog, first he must get used to doing it and overcome possible fears regarding the animal.

CTAC steps of treat-giving: This sequence sets out the gradual coming-together of participant and dog over time.

1. The RI tosses the treat to the dog several steps away without visual contact.

2. The RI tosses the treat to the dog several steps away with visual contact.

3. The RI puts the treat in the palm of the hand of the AIT, who is at a considerable distance from the dog.

4. The RI puts the treat in the AIT's palm while the technician is touching the dog's snout.

5. The RI places the treat on a tray and extends the tray to the dog.

6. The RI puts the treat on some part of his own body and the dog approaches to eat it.

7. The RI places the treat on his own palm and, with physical support from the AIT, gives it to the dog.

8. The RI places the treat on his palm and, without help, gives it to the dog.

9. The RI holds the treat between two fingers and, with the AIT's hand on his hand, gives it to the dog.

10. The RI holds the treat between two fingers and gives it to the dog without help.

Variations:

– To work on fine motor skills, we can have the RI pick up the treat with a clothespin and give it to the dog, or have him use a spoon.

COMMANDS FOR THE DOG	MATERIALS
• Stay	• Treats
• Treat	• Plates
• Look	• Trays
	• Clothespins

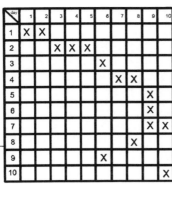

	Physical coordination	Objectives
Psychomotor Area	Sensory stimulation	• Exercise fine motor skills
	Space-time perception	• Exercise tactile perception
	Corporal awareness	• Exercise olfactory perception
Cognitive Area	Atention and concentration	• Express feelings
	Recognition of categories	• Develop an accurate and positive self-image
	Memory	• Create an affective bond
	Language and communication	• Allow closer relationships
Social-emotional Area	Presentation	
	Activity	
	Leave-taking and relaxation	
	Board games	

PSYCHO-MOTOR ACTIVITY

303

The objective of this activity is for the RI to get close to the dog and remain calm and relaxed.

If the RI shows signs of stress over the dog's presence, we take all the time we need to gradually reduce the distance between him and the dog.

– At no time should the RI feel cornered. He should always have the possibility of moving away from the animal.
– The dog should always be below the RI's line of sight.
– The dog remains stationary and calm, waiting for the RI to approach.
– The therapist is constantly aware of the RI's state of mind and guides the movement toward greater proximity.
– The AIT manages the dog and is the link between the RI and the animal.

We can use different strategies to begin to create a bond between the participant and the dog.

– With the dog lying down and relaxed, we play at tossing a ball between the RI (who is helped by the therapist) and the dog (who is helped by the technician.)
– The dog is in the "down" position and calm. We place next to him an object the RI likes so he gets close to the animal when he goes to get it.
– The RI and the IP each take an end of a leash of about six feet in length. The dog, along with the AIT, is waiting on the far side of the room. The IP and the RI sing a song that is relaxing to the RI, and they approach the dog slowly. When they reach the dog, the IP hooks the clip on to the dog's collar while the RI continues to hold the handle end.
– Trail of handkerchiefs that leads to the dog. The dog is seated. The RI follows a path of handkerchiefs, coming nearer the animal with each one he picks up. When he reaches the animal, he places the handkerchiefs on the dog's body, with or without the help of the AIT.
– Brushing. With the dog sitting on a chair, encourage the RI to brush him, maintaining whatever distance he is comfortable with.

COMMANDS FOR THE DOG	MATERIALS
• Sit	• Two-meter leash
• Down	• Balls
• Stay	• Hoops
• Crawl	• Handkerchiefs
	• Brush

		Objectives
Psychomotor Area	Physical coordination	
	Sensory stimulation	• Practice self-control
	Space-time perception	• Positive resolution of conflicts
	Corporal awareness	• Expression of feelings and emotions
Cognitive Area	Atention and concentration	• Verbal and non-verbal communication
	Recognition of categories	• Create affective bonds
	Memory	• Allow closer relationships
	Language and communication	• Foster positive group dynamic
Social-emotional Area	Presentation	
	Activity	
	Leave-taking and relaxation	
	Board games	

Passive walk with the CTAC anchoring belt.

We use a long leash and a padded anchoring belt with a ring at the level of the RI's navel to link the dog and the RI. These two elements allow us to encourage the RI to walk around without him in direct contact with the dog. Even so, there is a visual input, because the dog is in front of the RI.

Before beginning the exercise, we gradually get the RI used to using the anchoring belt. He is not allowed to put it on or take it off, these tasks being the exclusive reserve of the therapist.

The RI, linked to the dog by the leash, follows the dog at the speed maintained by the animal, which is in turn regulated by the AIT. The therapist walks beside the RI, pointing out to him the presence of the dog to focus the participant's attention there and provide visual stimulation during the walk.

Active walk with CTAC autism vest

For this we use the CTAC autism vest, which makes it easier for the RI to walk beside the dog.

The RI is linked to the dog by way of a leash that goes from the dog's harness to the ring on the side of the RI's anchoring belt.

As opposed to the previous exercise, here the RI performs an active role during the walk, employing a handle on the autism vest for taking control of the dog.

The RI's safety and sense of security are constantly protected:

– He must get used to holding the handle on the autism vest at all times
– He must stay by the dog's side during the walk.
– He must not unhook the anchoring mechanisms (belt and leash).

COMMANDS FOR THE DOG	MATERIALS
• Push	• Belt with central ring and two-meter leash
• Heel	• CTAC autism vest
• Stay	• Anchoring leashes: one-meter leash and belt with side ring

	Physical coordination	Objectives
Psychomotor Area	Sensory stimulation	• Exercise gross motor skills
	Space-time perception	• Learn and respect social norms
	Corporal awareness	• Discover elements of adult social life
Cognitive Area	Atention and concentration	• Foment group responsibility
	Recognition of categories	• Stimulate inter-group communication
	Memory	• Experiment the pleasure of movement
	Language and communication	• Experience the shedding of inhibitions
Social-emotional Area	Presentation	• Express feelings and emotions
	Activity	• Develop self-motivation
	Leave-taking and relaxation	• Create affective bonds
	Board games	

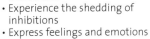

PSYCHO-MOTOR ACTIVITY

Active walk with leash and a transitional element

Sometimes during a walk, the RI has difficulty maintaining pressure on the handle of the leash. When this happens, we can help him by attaching to the leash handle something he knows and likes, or a piece of a texture he knows and likes, such as that of a hoop, a handkerchief or foam rubber. After a while of using that, we can sheathe the transitional element with a piece of material of the same texture as the leash handle.

Then when the RI feels secure in walking the dog along with the IP, we can remove the object. At this stage, every time the RI lets go of he leash, the IP must step in and motivate him to pick it up again, and help him do so if necessary.

The AIT will keep the dog a couple steps ahead of the RI so the tension on the leash is sufficient to motivate the RI to move forward, though not so much so as to prompt him to release the leash.

The RI walks the dog on his own.

Eventually, the RI will walk the dog on his own with a conventional leash. We can choose to begin the walk with the dog in the "heel" position between the RI and the AIT while linked by one leash to the RI and another to the AIT.

When it's clear the RI feels sure of himself, the AIT tells him he is letting go of his own leash and directs the RI to continue walking the dog on his own.

It's important for the dog to proceed in the "heel" position alongside the RI and the AIT.

COMMANDS FOR THE DOG	MATERIALS
• Stay	• Leashes
• Heel	• Transitional objects for RI

	Physical coordination	Objectives
Psychomotor Area	Sensory stimulation	• Exercise gross motor skills
	Space-time perception	• Exercise tactile perception
	Corporal awareness	• Mastery and control of body movements
Cognitive Area	Atention and concentration	• Acquire or exercise notion of space and direction
	Recognition of categories	• Pay attention to movements of others
	Memory	• Foster relationships of affinity
	Language and communication	• Experiment the pleasure of movement
Social-emotional Area	Presentation	• Exercise sight-body coordination
	Activity	
	Leave-taking and relaxation	
	Board games	

PSYCHO-MOTOR ACTIVITY

The objective of this activity is to be able to walk the therapy dog or dogs when the number of RIs is greater than the number of dogs.

Exercise 1:

We can attach more than one leash to the dog's collar so that a few RIs can walk the same dog simultaneously. The leashes can be of different lengths and colors so as to be able to work on instructions during the walk, such as: "Grab the long red leash."

The RIs can always take turns walking the dog, passing the leashes to another participant who has not yet held one.

Exercise 2:

With one dog and a very long leash we can take a walk with several RIs at the same time. We attach the leash to the dog's collar and invite the RIs to take hold of it at different points, keeping a certain distance between each other. We can also mark where we want them to take hold by making knots in the leash or tying on handkerchiefs at intervals.

The AIT will hold the leash at a point some 20 centimeters (about 8 inches) above the collar to prevent the RIs from putting too much pressure on the dog's neck.

Exercise 3:

Run a handkerchief through the leash handle. We ask two RIs to each take hold of an end of the handkerchief. They can now walk the dog together, but must collaborate to do so.

Exercise 4:

Pass a certain number of different colored hoops through the leash handle. The RIs will each take hold of a hoop, with the color for each one determined by a toss of the colors die.

COMMANDS FOR THE DOG	MATERIALS
• Tug • Heel ✍	• Leashes of different lengths and colors • Long leash • Hoops • Handkerchiefs • Colors die

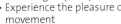

		Objectives
Psychomotor Area	Physical coordination	• Exercise gross motor skills • Exercise fine motor skills • Imitate movements: mastery and control of body movements • Pay attention to movements of others • Foment socialization • Stimulate physical contact and interaction • Accept norms of social interaction • Foment group cooperation • Experience the pleasure of movement
	Sensory stimulation	
	Space-time perception	
	Corporal awareness	
Cognitive Area	Atention and concentration	
	Recognition of categories	
	Memory	
	Language and communication	
Social-emotional Area	Presentation	
	Activity	
	Leave-taking and relaxation	
	Board games	

The objective of this activity is for the RI to work with the concept of left and right by placing hoops on the dog's body.

We place six hoops around the room – three red ones and three blue – and we ask the RI to pick one up and place it on a certain part of the dog, for example: red hoops on the left legs, blue hoops on the right legs. So the left side of the dog is the red side, and the right side the blue side. Then we ask the RI to place the remaining red hoop on his left leg and the remaining blue one on his right leg.

Variations:

– Interactive die of body parts; right-left. The RI tosses the die and must attach a piece of red or blue adhesive to the body part that came up on the die, with the IP saying whether it should the 'right' or 'left' of that part.

– Sequence of tricks. The IP makes up a series of cards representing some of these tricks: Right shake (paw); left shake (paw); Mark, left; Mark, right; Right twist; Left twist.

We lay out a circuit and the RI must reach the finish ine following the instructions regarding left and right given to him by the IP. He does this by using the command 'Mark,' extending the correct hand for the dog to touch with his snout, or the command 'Peek -a- boo,' with the dog passing beneath either the left or right leg. If the selection of the hand or leg is correct, the dog marks or passes under and the RI advances toward the finish line.

COMMANDS FOR THE DOG	MATERIALS
• Stand	• Colored hoops
• Stay	• Colored adhesives
• Mark	• CTAC interactive die
• Paw (right and left)	
• Peek-a-boo (right and left)	
• Twist (right and left)	

		Objectives
Psychomotor Area	Physical coordination	• Develop mental image of body structure
	Sensory stimulation	• Acquire or exercise notion of symmetry
	Space-time perception	• Codification and de-codification of symbols
	Corporal awareness	• Improve language comprehension and expression
Cognitive Area	Atention and concentration	• Work on concept of right and left
	Recognition of categories	
	Memory	
	Language and communication	
Social-emotional Area	Presentation	
	Activity	
	Leave-taking and relaxation	
	Board games	

PSYCHO-MOTOR ACTIVITY

313

The objective of this activity is to get the RI to use his force of traction. To do so, we have a variety of exercises.

Exercise 1:

We place the dog on a small-wheeled cart or wagon that is attached to a cord or leash. The RI, walking backward, pulls the cart from one side of the room to the other.

Exercise 2:

We invite the RI to play a tugging game with the dog. The dog grips a toy with his mouth while the RI grips it in his hands, and they pull in opposite directions.

Exercise 3:

With the dog lying on his side, we place a large colored kerchief or a flat strap beneath his upper body. The RI must pull the kerchief out from under the dog while the IP applies resistance on the other end. When the RI succeeds in extracting the kerchief, he ties it around the dog's neck. If a strap is used, a card can be attached to the far end with a word the RI must read or an activity he must describe when he completes his task.

Exercise 4:

Walking a dog who tugs on the leash. We invite the RI to take the dog for a walk, but with a dog who will tug on the leash (acting like he wants to pull away). The RI applies the force necessary to regain control of the walks. The AIT, following the instructions of the therapist, at all times controls the amount of force exerted by the dog.

Exercise 5:

To work on arm extension and flexibility. The RI is standing squarely on two feet next to the IP. We give him the handle of a leash attached to a dog who walks in a circle around him, exerting varying degrees of tension on the line.

COMMANDS FOR THE DOG	MATERIALS
• Get it	• Cart or wagon
• Stay	• Round cord or leash
• Push, pull	• Flat strap or leash
• Back	• Kerchiefs
• Down	• Cards

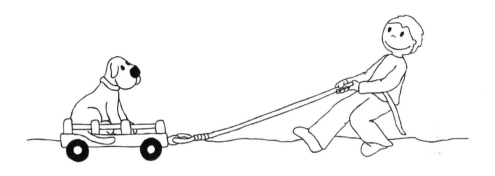

	Physical coordination	Objectives
Psychomotor Area	Sensory stimulation	• Exercise gross motor skills
	Space-time perception	• Exercise fine motor skills • Develop and control muscular
	Corporal awareness	strength
Cognitive Area	Atention and concentration	• Experience the pleasure of achievement
	Recognition of categories	
	Memory	
	Language and communication	
Social-emotional Area	Presentation	
	Activity	
	Leave-taking and relaxation	
	Board games	

PSYCHO-MOTOR ACTIVITY

315

WORKING WITH CONTAINERS

The objective of these exercises is to get the RI to use fine motor skills to open and close different kinds of jars and receptacles, to be able to fill them with dry dog food or to be able to feed the dog.

Exercise 1:

We will be using Kong®-brand dog toys, which we'll ask the RI to fill, with the idea of giving them to the dog at the end of the session. Thanks to the different shapes of these toys and the variety of materials that can be used to fill them, we can regulate the degree of difficulty of the activity.

Exercise 2:

We work with children's stackable colored barrels because they're easy to open and close. Also, the dog can eat directly from them. We set out several closed barrels, some of them empty and some with food inside. The RI goes along picking each one up and shaking it to hear whether there is food inside. If there is, he opens it and gives it to the dog.

Exercise 3:

We have several types of containers with different means of closure. Inside each one we place an item the RI can use to interact with the dog: a ball, treats, a brush, a leash. We also place inside each one a note for the RI with an instruction, such as, "touch the dog's head," or "command the dog to sit."

Exercise 4:

Give the dog food with a spoon or a clothespin. The dog is placed in front of the RI, either sitting or lying down. We invite the RI to feed the dog with either a spoon or a clothespin. In the latter case, he must use both hands to secure the nugget with the clothespin.

COMMANDS FOR THE DOG	MATERIALS
• Stay	• Colored barrels
• Down	• Jars
• Treat	• Treats
• Various tricks and skills	• Balls
	• Skills cards
	• Spoon
	• Clothespins

	Physical coordination	Objectives
Psychomotor Area	Sensory stimulation	• Exercise fine motor skills
	Space-time perception	• Exercise tactile perception
	Corporal awareness	• Exercise sense of smell
Cognitive Area	Atention and concentration	• Develop and control muscle strength
	Recognition of categories	• Pay attention to instructions
	Memory	• Exercise listening skills
	Language and communication	• Increase tolerance for frustration
Social-emotional Area	Presentation	• Exercise eye-body coordination
	Activity	
	Leave-taking and relaxation	
	Board games	

PSYCHO-MOTOR ACTIVITY

The objective of this activity is for the RI to express and verbalize his feelings.

We exhibit some illustrated cards to the dog and the RI explains what they show. The dog listens attentively, then expresses his mood by way of vocalizations (barks, howls, whines...) or by way of gestures that indicate, for example, shyness (covers his eyes with a paw), submission (lying down belly-up), fear (near prostration with the head touching the floor), happiness (spinning in circles), etc.

Next, the IP tells a story to the RI, who in turn tells the dog how a person would feel in such a situation. Those same feelings he must now express vocally: with laughter, shouts, crying... and with gestures: folding his arms, raising his arms, covering his face...The dog closely observes all this and will try to imitate the expressions to the best of his ability.

Our silhouette:

We place two sheets of paper on the floor, one horizontally and the other vertically.

We're going to have the RI to draw an outline of a dog on one and an outline of himself on the other. First we have the dog lie down on the horizontal sheet and the RI traces his outline with a pen or a marker. He then decorates that drawing with words or images that express his feelings about the dog, the therapy sessions or the dog's own feelings.

Then we ask him to lie down on his outline, and we have the dog lie down next to him. The IP draws an outline of the two together, which the RI will, with the help of the IP, decorate that drawing with words or sketches expressing what he most likes about himself, his body, the way he acts, the things he likes, his relationship with the dog, etc.

COMMANDS FOR THE DOG	MATERIALS
• Kiss	• Cards
• No!	• Chalk or markers
• Belly	
• Hide	
• Beg	
• Crawl	
• Back	
• Twist	
• Shame	
• Speak	
• Down	

			Objectives
Psychomotor Area	Physical coordination		• Control mobility and flexibility of the mouth and facial features
	Sensory stimulation		
	Space-time perception		• Control facial gestures and moderate tone of voice
	Corporal awareness		• Learn to listen, respond and imitate
Cognitive Area	Atention and concentration		• Express feelings: sadness, happiness, anger
	Recognition of categories		
	Memory		• Express one's own personality and manage emotions and feelings
	Language and communication		
Social-emotional Area	Presentation		
	Activity		
	Leave-taking and relaxation		
	Board games		

socialization exercises

socialization

exercises

The objective of this game is for the RIs to remain in contact and still in groups of at least two.

We introduce this game showing them and describing different materials that can be used for making a statue.

The RIs name a material and the dog takes it to them in his mouth or in a basket so they can touch it and compare its properties to those of other materials.

Then we tell them that now we are going to make statues and that they will help using their own bodies. They will work in couples so as to be able to create a more elaborate statue.

We can make suggestions regarding their subject by way of body posture, positioning them one way or another, or verbally offering ideas such as: What would a statue of two friends meeting again after a long time look like? What would a statue of a soccer player about to score a goal look like? A statue of a train? Of a horse?

When the statue is finished, the dog will pass through the hollow parts to test the work's solidness. If it does not break or move, the work will be considered a success and the dog gets a treat.

We can ask the participants to describe the statues made by their companions.

At the end of the session, all the participants gather in a circle with their arms around each others' shoulders like in a football huddle. The dog will be in the middle and the kids must prevent him from getting out until the therapist gives the order. Then they all spread their legs so the dog can exit.

COMMANDS FOR THE DOG	MATERIALS
• Get it	• Cards showing statues
• Stay	• Marble
• Come	• Wood
	• Clay
	• Plaster
	• Chair

		Objectives
Psychomotor Area	Physical coordination	• Exercise sense of touch
	Sensory stimulation	• Exercise sense of place in space
	Space-time perception	• Exercise balance
	Corporal awareness	• Develop and control muscular strength
Cognitive Area	Atention and concentration	• Control movements
	Recognition of categories	• Acquire or exercise symbolic thinking
	Memory	• Acquire or exercise ability to concentrate
	Language and communication	• Improve oral comprehension
Social-emotional Area	Presentation	• Acquire or exercise notion of geometric shapes
	Activity	• Stimulate the imagination
	Leave-taking and relaxation	• Stimulate socialization
	Board games	• Foster trust in others

THE STORY OF FEELINGS

The objective is for the RI to act out emotions described in a story.

The IP writes a story about the life of the therapy dog with episodes and incidents of great emotional content.

Sitting next to the dog, the IP reads the story aloud and the RI must act out the emotions present in the narrative, with the aid of the dog.

We're working here with feelings, including happiness, sadness, shame, doubt, anger, and with actions such as laughing, hugging, jumping up and down, caressing...

Variations:

– We give the RI a map of the "City of feelings." We use chalk to draw on the floor a diagram resembling the map. The RI, accompanied by the dog, follows arrows around the "city." At each street he comes to, he must act out the emotion or action indicated by the street name: "Street of Hugs," "Sadness Street," "Street of Song," etc.

COMMANDS FOR THE DOG	MATERIALS
• Shame	• Story with emotions
• Hide	• City map
• Jump	
• Kiss	
• Bang	
• Stay	

324

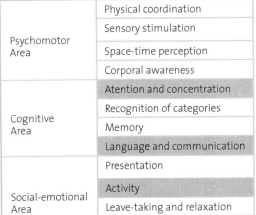

	Physical coordination	Objectives
Psychomotor Area	Sensory stimulation	• Acquire or exercise symbolic thinking
	Space-time perception	• Improve oral comprehension
	Corporal awareness	• Stimulate creativity and different ways of thinking
Cognitive Area	Atention and concentration	• Stimulate the imagination
	Recognition of categories	• Stimulate active listening
	Memory	
	Language and communication	
Social-emotional Area	Presentation	
	Activity	
	Leave-taking and relaxation	
	Board games	

WELCOME

The objective of this game is for the RIs to enjoy the applause of their companions.

The RIs are seated in a semicircle in the room awaiting the arrival of the IP and the dog.

When they enter, they take their place in front of the "audience" and receive a round of enthusiastic applause, which they acknowledge by both taking a bow.

Then, one by one, the RI takes the dog's leash, exits the room with him and comes back in. The participants receive him with heartfelt applause, which the RI responds to in the manner he sees fit.

He then hands the dog off to one of his companions, and the sequence is repeated.

Variations:

– We introduce the concept of greeting between the two participants when the dog is passed from one to the other.

COMMANDS FOR THE DOG	MATERIALS
• Walk together • Sit	• Treats

	Physical coordination	Objectives
Psychomotor Area	Sensory stimulation	• Develop social interaction
	Space-time perception	• Stimulate socialization
	Corporal awareness	• Learn and follow social norms
Cognitive Area	Atention and concentration	• Introductions and greetings
	Recognition of categories	• Create a welcoming environment, a stress-free one that encourages listening with the goal of being together
	Memory	• Experience the pleasure of laughter
	Language and communication	• Experience "letting go" of inhibitions
Social-emotional Area	Presentation	• Promote propitious environment for group
	Activity	
	Leave-taking and relaxation	
	Board games	

RITUAL GREETINGS

The objective of this game is to help the participants relate to each other cordially and correctly when greeting or being introduced.

If possible, each of the RIs will have a therapy dog he will walk in the "heel" position.

They all walk around the room, and every time a dog sits down the RIs must greet each other, varying the form of greeting as the game continues: shaking hands, slapping five, embracing, pat on the shoulder, waving, kissing on the cheek, a nod of the head, hands together as if in prayer, with a "thumbs up," etc. When the dog stands, they resume walking around until the next dog sits, when the greetings are repeated.

If there is more than one dog, the IP will determine the order in which the dogs sit, and will give the commands from where he is observing the exercise.

Variations:

— If we don't have enough dogs for everybody, we form two groups. In one group, everyone has a dog, in the other, no one has a dog. When a dog sits, the participants in both groups approach each other and make their greetings, after which the dog is handed over to the person who didn't have one before.

— If we have only one dog, we form a big circle. The IP says (for example): "Step forward whoever is wearing blue glasses." That person approaches the IP, they greet each other, and the therapist hands the dog over to him. This continues until everyone in the group has had a turn.

— The greetings can be accompanied and expanded with a brief verbal exchange of everyday pleasantries.

COMMANDS FOR THE DOG	MATERIALS
• Stay	• Treats
• Sit	• Wheel of ritual greetings
• Down	

	Physical coordination	Objectives
Psychomotor Area	Sensory stimulation	• Acquire or exercise the ability to concentrate
	Space-time perception	• Develop skills of observation
	Corporal awareness	• Stimulate group communication and interaction
Cognitive Area	Atention and concentration	• Stimulate active listening
	Recognition of categories	• Encourage sense of fairness, giving each his turn
	Memory	• Listen without interrupting
	Language and communication	
Social-emotional Area	Presentation	
	Activity	
	Leave-taking and relaxation	
	Board games	

WHO'S IT BEHIND?

The objective of this game is for the RIs to discover which of them has gotten a prize from the dog.

Each of the RIs makes himself a rattle by putting different materials in a bottle.

The IP begins the exercise by shaking his rattle and the RIs close or cover their eyes.

The IP, accompanied by the dog, circulates among or around the RIs and at some point, without giving himself away, leaves a bowl with treats behind one of them.

When he stops shaking his rattle, the RIs open their eyes and turn around to see which of them has the bowl of treats behind him.

He gets to give the dog a treat, but first he must have him do a trick or perform a skill. Then it is he who shakes his rattle and the next round begins, with the IP circulating with the dog and deciding where to leave the bowl.

At the end, we can ask the RIs one by one to recall and name the trick he had the dog perform, or ask them which trick a companion chose.

Variations:

– Taking turns, each RI shakes his rattle while the dog circulates among them. When that RI stops making the noise, the dog barks behind one of the participants. The others must guess which one the dog is behind. Then it is that participant's turn to shake his rattle.

– Give out the materials for the rattles on a tray. The RIs must follow instructions in selecting the materials and putting them in the bottle.

COMMANDS FOR THE DOG	MATERIALS
• Sit	• Dark bottles with screw-on caps
• Speak	• Rice
• Treat	• Pebbles
• Various tricks and skills	• Small shapes of pasta
	• Sand
	• Skills cards
	• Skills die

	Physical coordination	Objectives
Psychomotor Area	Sensory stimulation	• Exercise fine motor skills
	Space-time perception	• Exercise auditory perception and rhythm
	Corporal awareness	• Stimulate socialization
Cognitive Area	Atention and concentration	• Stimulate group communication and interaction
	Recognition of categories	• Accept norms of social interaction
	Memory	• Experience the pleasure or achievement
	Language and communication	• Experience the pleasure or guessing correctly
Social-emotional Area	Presentation	
	Activity	
	Leave-taking and relaxation	
	Board games	

SOCIALIZATION

FIND THE BALL

The objective of this game is for the dog to find a hidden ball and show us where it is by using his snout or paw.

The RIs sit in a circle and pass a ball around, saying the name of the companion they pass it to or following another instruction given by the IP.

When the IP claps his hands, the person who has the ball must hide it somewhere on his body. The IP commands the dog to look for the ball. The dog goes from one RI to the other, sniffing, and sits down in front of the one with the ball.

This game can be combined with another we call, "Fists of the Superheroes." The RIs pass the ball and when the IP gives the signal, all the players thrust their fists toward the center of the circle. The dog goes around sniffing all the fists and sits in front of the person with the ball.

At the end of the exercise, the RIs make a tighter circle so that, sitting down, their knees touch. They wrap up the session by passing a small dog from one to another, each one cuddling him, petting him and saying good-bye with words of affection.

Variations:

– We use three bowls, ones that can be different from each other or all the same. We hide a ball under one. The RI must guess which bowl the ball is under, with or without help from the dog.

COMMANDS FOR THE DOG	MATERIALS
• Sit	• Small ball
• Stay	• Bowls, different or alike
• Head down	
• Mark	

	Physical coordination	Objectives
Psychomotor Area	Sensory stimulation	• Exercise fine motor skills
	Space-time perception	• Learn companions' names • Exercise hand-eye coordination
	Corporal awareness	• Exercise visual perception
Cognitive Area	Atention and concentration	• Pay attention to movements of others
	Recognition of categories	• Develop language comprehension and expression
	Memory	• Develop social interaction
	Language and communication	• Encourage sense of fairness, giving all participants turns of equal time
Social-emotional Area	Presentation	• Learn and respect social norms
	Activity	
	Leave-taking and relaxation	
	Board games	

SOCIALIZATION

The objective of this game is for the RI to listen attentively to a narrative and then answer a series of questions.

We invent a "life story" for one of the therapy dogs the RI works with at the center and with which he has a particularly strong emotional bond. The story should be as rich in detail as possible, given the capabilities of the group.

The dog will be seated next to the RI to foster contact between them. The IP reads the story aloud, which can also be read by the RI.

When the reading is over, the dog fetches a basket and carries it to the RI in his mouth. The basket contains cards with questions about the narrative of the dog's life, and the RI must correctly answer the questions.

With every right answer, the dog does a trick that the RI likes. If the answer is not correct, the dog remains still, or performs an action meaning "wrong."

Variations:

– The questions can be hidden throughout an obstacle course to be completed by the RI after the reading of the story.

COMMANDS FOR THE DOG	MATERIALS
• Down	• Dog's story
• Stay	• Cards with questions
• Fetch	• Basket
• Carry	
• No	
• Pleasing tricks and skills	

	Physical coordination	Objectives
Psychomotor Area	Sensory stimulation	• Improve oral comprehension
	Space-time perception	• Develop language comprehension and expression
	Corporal awareness	• Encourage reading
Cognitive Area	Atention and concentration	• Stimulate active listening
	Recognition of categories	• Enhance short-term memory
	Memory	• Enhance long-term memory
	Language and communication	
Social-emotional Area	Presentation	
	Activity	
	Leave-taking and relaxation	
	Board games	

GROUP INTRODUCTION

The objective of this activity is to introduce the dog and the RIs to each other in a relaxed and stress-free way and make the first contact between them a pleasant experience.

The participants sit in a circle or a semi-circle. The IP introduces himself to the group saying his own name, that of the dog and adding some information that can be either important, funny or simple social banter. Then the RIs take turns telling the dog their name, to which the animal responds with a greeting or a trick.

The IP approaches the RIs with the dog, and walks him slowly around so each one can touch or stroke his back without having the dog's face too close to his own.

With those RIs who feel calm and comfortable near the dog, the animal can sit or lie down in front of him and receive a treat.

The IP makes sure that each RI gets the same amount of interaction time with the dog. To that end, he has the dog move around or sit or stand quietly at different points.

Variations:

– One by one the RIs take their place in front of the group with the dog and introduce themselves to their session mates, saying their name and saying whether or not they have or have had a pet. The group's members must pay attention, as the order in which they introduce themselves may have been previously established, or it may be determined by way of responses to questions about what the other members have already said. When each one is finished, he gives the dog a treat and hands him over to the next speaker.

– The RIs take seats around a table, each one with a treat in his hand. The dog is on the table, waiting for one of them to give him a treat. We go around the table, with each RI saying the name of the companion to his right until the IP claps his hands. When that happens, the person whose name was just said gives his treat to the dog.

COMMANDS FOR THE DOG	MATERIALS
• Sit • Down • Treat • Get it	• Treats

	Physical coordination	Objectives
Psychomotor Area	Sensory stimulation	• Acquire or exercise the ability to concentrate
	Space-time perception	• Develop observational skill
	Corporal awareness	• Stimulate group communication and interaction
Cognitive Area	Atention and concentration	• Stimulate active listening
	Recognition of categories	• Ensure fairness, giving each person equal time
	Memory	• Learn to listen without interruption
	Language and communication	
Social-emotional Area	Presentation	
	Activity	
	Leave-taking and relaxation	
	Board games	

SOCIALIZATION

FIND THE TREAT

The objective of this game is for the dog to find out who among the participants has a treat hidden in his pocket.

Seated in a circle or a semi-circle, the RIs tell the dog that one of them is going to hide a treat in his pocket and that he must guess which one it is.

The dog and the IP handling him leave the room. The therapist stays with the RIs, seated on the floor.

One of the RIs puts a treat in his pocket. When the dog comes back in, he moves around the group sniffing and studying each individual. Then he goes to the person hiding the treat and lays his head on his lap, waiting calmly for that person to give him the treat. (The therapist has indicated to the IP/handler by a previously agreed upon signal which of the RIs has the treat.)

Variations:

– We leave the dog lying in the center of the circle and the IP leaves the room. One of the RIs ties a kerchief around the dog's neck and goes back to his place. The IP comes back in and must guess who put the kerchief on the dog.

COMMANDS FOR THE DOG	MATERIALS
• Sit	• Treats
• Down	• Handkerchief
• Stay	
• Find	
• Head down	
• Treat	

	Physical coordination	Objectives
Psychomotor Area	Sensory stimulation	• Get used to the dog being near
	Space-time perception	• Stimulate trust in others • Discover the fun in being surprised
	Corporal awareness	• Learn to await one's turn
Cognitive Area	Atention and concentration	• Accept norms of social interaction
	Recognition of categories	
	Memory	
	Language and communication	
Social-emotional Area	Presentation	
	Activity	
	Leave-taking and relaxation	
	Board games	

SOCIALIZATION

TREAT BOX

The objective of this game is for the RIs to realize that the music has stopped while they're engaged in another activity.

The players, seated in a circle around the dog, pass a jar of treats around while the music is playing.

When the music stops, the one holding the jar must open it and take out as many treats as the therapist tells him to.

Before giving the dog a treat, he can interact in some fashion with him (pet him, have him do a trick, etc.)

Variations:

– The RIs pass around jars previously prepared with the essence of different fragrances, one at a time. When the music stops, the one holding the jar tries to identify the aroma. (If necessary, the thing that naturally gives off that fragrance can be in the jar along with the concentrated essence, to make the identification easier.)

– When the RI names the thing that gives off that smell, the dog takes him that thing. The RI takes it from him and gives the dog a treat.

COMMANDS FOR THE DOG	MATERIALS
• Various tricks and skills	• Non-transparent jars
• Fetch	• Jars with aromas
• Carry	• Source of music
• Drop	• Skills die

	Physical coordination	Objectives
Psychomotor Area	Sensory stimulation	• Exercise the sense of smell
	Space-time perception	• Exercise auditory perception and discrimination
	Corporal awareness	• Exercise sense of rhythm
Cognitive Area	Atention and concentration	• Acquire or exercise ability to concentrate
	Recognition of categories	• Recognize objects
	Memory	• Enrich vocabulary
	Language and communication	• Stimulate group communication and interaction
Social-emotional Area	Presentation	• Experience the pleasure of guessing correctly
	Activity	
	Leave-taking and relaxation	
	Board games	

SOCIALIZATION

341

MY FRIENDS' NAMES

The objective of this game is for the RIs to remember the names of their session mates.

The participants form a circle and sit down. The IP, who is with the dog in the center, makes the introductions. Then he approaches one of the RIs, who must say his own name and that of the person to his left and to his right.

If he does this correctly, he goes to the center of the circle where he spends a few minutes with the dog, petting him, perhaps putting a kerchief on him.

Then he approaches another RI, who says his name and those of the players on either side of him.

Variations:

– The RI must remember the names of the various dogs taking part in the session. He tosses the colors die and must say the name of the dog wearing the kerchief of the color that came up. If he is correct, he gets to interact with the dog.

– The IP can show the RIs a diagram of the dog's family tree to help them talk about and draw their own. The dog can help by taking pictures of relatives to them, and the RIs say the names of those people.

– Recall and say the names of classmates. The dog takes photos to them, and the RI says the names.

COMMANDS FOR THE DOG	MATERIALS
• Sit	• Treats
• Stay	• Colors die
• Heel	• Handkerchiefs
• Treat	
• Various tricks and skills	

	Physical coordination	Objectives
Psychomotor Area	Sensory stimulation	• Develop social interaction
	Space-time perception	• Stimulate group communication and interaction
	Corporal awareness	• Introductions
Cognitive Area	Atention and concentration	• Stimulate active listening
	Recognition of categories	• Learn to listen and respond
	Memory	• Stimulate communication between groups
	Language and communication	
Social-emotional Area	Presentation	
	Activity	
	Leave-taking and relaxation	
	Board games	

SOCIALIZATION

THE DOG PHONE

The objective of this game is for the RI to carry out an order given by the IP that the individuals in the group have passed along by whispering in the next person's ear.

The members of the group form a semi-circle. The IP positions a dog in front of them.

The dog goes over to the first person and "whispers" a phrase or directive into his ear (relayed by the IP). He could also give the directive by showing an illustrated card or a written message.

The message is then transmitted "in secret" down the line, whispering into the ear of the next person or acting out the action ordered by the IP ("touch his nose," "hug him," "blow puffs of air on him," etc.)

When the IP claps his hands, the RI who has just received the message goes over to the dog, which is seated before the group, and does what has been ordered.

Variations:

– The IP stands or sits beside the dog in the center of the semi-circle and tells the group what the dog has decided they must do all at the same time, either to themselves or to the person beside them.

– Taking turns, each one says an action to be performed with the dog. Then, after all have spoken, one by one they get up and do with the dog whatever action they said.

COMMANDS FOR THE DOG	MATERIALS
• Mark the ear • Stay • Sit • Down • Give 	• Actions cards • Actions phrases

344

		Objectives
Psychomotor Area	Physical coordination	• Develop mental image of body structure • Listen to instructions • Pay attention to movements of others • Acquire or exercise ability to imitate • Develop or evaluate short-term memory • Develop social interaction • Stimulate socialization • Stimulate physical contact and interaction
	Sensory stimulation	
	Space-time perception	
	Corporal awareness	
Cognitive Area	Atention and concentration	
	Recognition of categories	
	Memory	
	Language and communication	
Social-emotional Area	Presentation	
	Activity	
	Leave-taking and relaxation	
	Board games	

SOCIALIZATION

OUR FEELINGS

The objective of this game is to compare the RI's emotions with those of the dog, and to act them out.

The IP poses questions. How do certain situations make us feel? How do we show how we feel with our bodies and our faces?

We describe different situations and ask the RI to try to act out how each one makes him feel.

At the same time, we show the RI photos or drawings of a dog whose body posture or face is a reaction to a certain stimulus. We observe the dog's body language and talk about why he might be feeling that particular emotion.

Then the game begins: the dog takes the RI one of the illustrated cards showing a dog emotion; he has to say which one it is, then select from the human-emotions cards the one corresponding to the dog's. Finally, he acts out that emotion.

Variations:

– The IP describes a situation in which the dog plays a role. We have two hoops on the floor, and in one we place the card illustrating one dog emotion and in the other we place its opposite. The dog goes to stand in one of the hoops, and the RI must say if that's the one with the emotion described by the IP.

– We can do the same with hoops and the human-emotions cards. The IP tells a story and the RI must go stand in the hoop corresponding to the emotion described in the story. The dog barks if he is correct.

COMMANDS FOR THE DOG	MATERIALS
• Stay	• Dog emotions cards
• Speak	• Human emotions cards
• Hide	• Hoops
• Kiss	
• Shame	
• Yuck	
• Back	
• Crawl	
• Head down	

  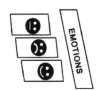

		Objectives
Psychomotor Area	Physical coordination	• Express feelings: sadness, happiness, anger
	Sensory stimulation	• Act together, cooperate
	Space-time perception	• Express fantasies
	Corporal awareness	• Express one's personality
Cognitive Area	Atention and concentration	• Experience the shedding of inhibitions
	Recognition of categories	• Explore different forms of communication: mime, rhythmic, figurative, theatrical
	Memory	
	Language and communication	
Social-emotional Area	Presentation	
	Activity	
	Leave-taking and relaxation	
	Board games	

SOCIALIZATION

RESPECT FOR DIVERSITY

The objective of this game is to help the RI realize that we are all different from each other and to encourage respect for diversity.

We place two or more dogs before the RI or a group of RIs. After we introduce each animal, the RIs comment on the physical differences among between them. The IP is at a blackboard, making a list of characteristics in columns beneath the name of each dog.

We can work on this same concept using other games. For example, the dogs can take turns carrying to each RI a basket containing cards inscribed with different characteristics. The RI picks a card and then places it on the bed of the dog that most resembles the description on the card (or he can clip the card on the right dog with a clothespin). Another option is for one of the dogs to touch with his snout or paw a card from among a display, and the RI then attaches that card to the dog with that characteristic.

Then we can move to noting the physical differences between the RIs. Each RI stands next to a dog and says out loud one of his own physical traits. The IP writes that on the blackboard beneath his name. We can also use the dog in this phase: he picks a "trait" card from a basket, and all those among the RIs who think they have that physical trait get up and stand next to the dog.

The message is that we all have different characteristics and we must respect each other for who we are.

Variations:

– We employ the same dynamic, but with more personal attributes: what makes us happy and what makes us sad or angry, our character, our preferences, etc.

COMMANDS FOR THE DOG	MATERIALS
• Stay	• Cards of physical characteristics
• Carry	• Comparative cards
• Stand	• Clothespins
• Mark	• Construction paper
• Pick	
• Get it	

	Physical coordination	Objectives
Psychomotor Area	Sensory stimulation	• Acquire or exercise the ability to concentrate
	Space-time perception	• Acquire or exercise basic concepts of size
	Corporal awareness	• Recognize the characteristics of objects
Cognitive Area	Atention and concentration	• Establish relationships between objects
	Recognition of categories	• Develop observational skills
	Memory	• Develop language: comprehension and expression
	Language and communication	• Stimulate active listening
Social-emotional Area	Presentation	• Experience the pleasure of achievement
	Activity	
	Leave-taking and relaxation	
	Board games	

The objective of this game is to reach the top of an oversized game board by correctly answering questions about dogs.

The IP draws up a list of 10 questions in each of four categories, each of which is represented by a color. For example, blue cards have questions about the dog's diet; red ones are about his anatomy; green ones deal with habits and behavior and yellow ones relate to his health and wellbeing.

We use chalk to draw a grid on the floor, four across and ten down. At the top of each column we place a photograph of a dog trick or skill that the RI can have the animal perform if he reaches the top of that column.

Each RI has a "bone" marker and, with the dog's help, advances up the column by correctly answering questions brought to him by the dog. The RI spins a wheel or tosses the colors die and, depending on what comes up, the dog brings him a question from the basket corresponding to that color.

If the answer is correct, the dog advances the bone one square in the column of that color. The RI continues answering questions until he reaches the top of one of the columns: the goal. The dog then takes him the same number of treats as questions he has correctly answered (in all the categories), and the RI has him perform the trick or skill at the top of the winning column.

Variations:

– We can modify the question categories in order to work on different areas of therapy.

COMMANDS FOR THE DOG	MATERIALS
• Sit	• Four decks of thematic cards
• Stay	• Chalk
• Fetch	• Dog abilities cards
• Carry	• Colors roulette wheel or die

	Physical coordination	Objectives
Psychomotor Area	Sensory stimulation	• Acquire or exercise ability to concentrate
	Space-time perception	• Improve oral comprehension
	Corporal awareness	• Stimulate group communication and interaction
Cognitive Area	Atention and concentration	• Develop social interaction
	Recognition of categories	• Learn and respect social norms
	Memory	• Stimulate active listening
	Language and communication	• Experience the pleasure of achievement
Social-emotional Area	Presentation	• Experience the pleasure of guessing correctly
	Activity	
	Leave-taking and relaxation	
	Board games	

SOCIALIZATION

SHERLOCK DOG

The objective of this activity is for the RIs to guess which dog is hidden inside a travel crate.

To begin, the AIT explains how the game works and introduces his therapy dogs. He describes each one in detail: coat type, tail type, weight, sex, color, etc.

Then he has the RIs turn their backs and he puts one of the dogs in the travel crate and escorts the others out of the room.

The RIs now take turns asking questions about the dog in the crate – with or without the aid of cards – to which the AIT gives only a yes-or-no answer.

Each time a new characteristic is discovered, a review is made of all those found out up to that point.

When it finally becomes clear which dog is in the crate, one of the RIs opens it, lets the dog out and pets him.

Variations:

– Use cards illustrating dog breeds in a guessing game. One of our dogs has in his mouth, in a basket or in a pocket of his CTAC blanket a card showing a dog breed. The RIs, by taking turns asking questions about the breed, discover which one it is. Each time one correctly guesses a breed, he gets to interact with the dog.

COMMANDS FOR THE DOG	MATERIALS
• Down • Stay	• Canine travel crate • CTAC dog blanket • Cards with questions

	Physical coordination	Objectives
Psychomotor Area	Sensory stimulation	• Acquire or exercise the ability to concentrate
	Space-time perception	• Acquire or exercise the notion of numbers and quantity
	Corporal awareness	• Acquire or exercise notion of colors and sizes
Cognitive Area	Atention and concentration	• Synthesize the parts of a whole
	Recognition of categories	• Develop or evaluate short-term memory
	Memory	• Recognize the properties of objects
	Language and communication	• Codification and de-codification of symbols
Social-emotional Area	Presentation	• Learn the dogs' names
	Activity	• Develop social interaction
	Leave-taking and relaxation	• Learn and respect social norms
	Board games	

SOCIALIZATION

GOOD COMMUNICATION

The objective of this activity is for the RI to work on a series of skills or tricks with different therapy dogs.

We need at least two therapy dogs, each with his own character traits and level of training and abilities.

The AIT makes a brief introduction of the dogs, describing both the strong and weak points of their "personality." Then he asks the RIs to each mention a positive aspect of his or her own character.

Then we have the RIs select two or three cards from an array of canine abilities cards, depending on the number of animals taking part. The participants talk about these skills or tricks and the commands they must use to get the dog to perform them, keeping in mind the particular character of each dog and his level of training. The RIs can be given the chance to negotiate among themselves or with the IP to exchange one card for another.

The RI must decide the sequence of actions and commands he will use in getting a dog to perform a certain skill or trick. We allow him to work out his own communication strategy with each of the dogs.

Finally, when all the participating dogs have been asked to perform their skills or tricks, the IP asks questions about the dogs' learning process; Which of them understood you best? Which was the one you worked most effectively with, and why? Which one paid most attention?

COMMANDS FOR THE DOG

• Stay
• Various tricks and skills

MATERIALS

• Cards illustrating skills of varying difficulty

		Objectives
Psychomotor Area	Physical coordination	• Improve decision-making capabilities
	Sensory stimulation	• Learn to plan
	Space-time perception	• Practice self-control
	Corporal awareness	• Develop ability to understand others
Cognitive Area	Atention and concentration	• Experience the pleasure of achievement
	Recognition of categories	• Improve verbal expression
	Memory	• Explore differing means of communication
	Language and communication	• Exercise hand-eye coordination
Social-emotional Area	Presentation	
	Activity	
	Leave-taking and relaxation	
	Board games	

GRAB THE FLAG (OR THE DOG)

The objective of this game is for the RIs to act in pairs in grabbing a handkerchief or a dog.

First we "pick teams." Two RIs will each select a member of the group, who then chooses another member, and so on until the participants are divided into two teams of equal size.

The IP can change the "captains" of the teams.

Each of the team members is assigned a number or a color, so that there is one of each number or color on each team.

The AIT stands holding aloft a handkerchief midway between the two aligned teams and shouts out a number or a color. The RIs with that number or color run toward him trying to be the first to grab the handkerchief and run back to his own line, where he gets to interact with the dog.

Once the game's dynamic is well understood, we can liven it up some. Each player (one on each team) is assigned a dog trick (sit, roll over, twist, etc.). The AIT holds the dog midway between the two lines and calls out a trick.

The RIs assigned that trick run toward the middle and the fastest one grabs the dog's leash. He gets to command the dog to perform that trick.

Variations:

   – Instead of using colors or numbers, the AIT can call out a particular trait, such as "those who wear glasses," or "blond-haired ones" or "those whose name begins with T."

COMMANDS FOR THE DOG	MATERIALS
• Heel	• Leash
• Sit	• CTAC dog blanket
• Stay	• Abilities cards

356

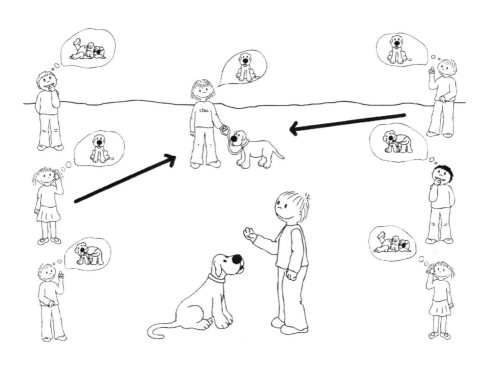

		Objectives
Psychomotor Area	Physical coordination	• Exercise overall dynamic coordination
	Sensory stimulation	• Pay attention to instructions
	Space-time perception	• Improve oral comprehension
	Corporal awareness	• Acquire or exercise auditory discrimination
Cognitive Area	Atention and concentration	• Develop or evaluate short-term memory
	Recognition of categories	• Develop social interaction
	Memory	• Respect social norms
	Language and communication	• Experience the pleasure of movement
Social-emotional Area	Presentation	• Create affective bonds
	Activity	• Develop self-motivational capability
	Leave-taking and relaxation	• Increase tolerance of frustration
	Board games	

VALES FOR TEACHING

The objective of this activity is to discuss and help the RI understand the challenges involved in teaching the dog skills, and what kinds of values – such as empathy, patience and respect – will help him succeed in this undertaking.

What better way to experience these values first-hand than by way of our affective bond with the dog?

We propose to the RI that he help us teach the dog a new skill, or teach him to disobey a given command.

The RI must transmit self-assuredness to the dog, planning the sequence of steps in the process and maintaining consistency. Above all, he must base the lesson on positive values if he wants the dog to learn and respond, and that both he and the animal enjoy the experience.

Empathy: The capacity to participate in the feelings of another being. In this case, the RI must recognize and understand the dog's emotions during the training process and be able to share those emotions in order to act accordingly.

Patience: A virtue that involves knowing how to wait for what one wants, despite setbacks or the prospect of sustained effort. It involves tolerating frustration and acceptance of the possibility that the dog might not be able to master a particular skill in the short, or the long run, no matter how much we want to teach him it.

Respect: This means concern for the rights of others, even if that interferes with one's own rights; keeping in mind the feelings of others, and acting accordingly.

COMMANDS FOR THE DOG	MATERIALS
• No! • Stay • Head down • Shame • Crawl • Look • Various skills and tricks 	• Skills cards

	Physical coordination	Objectives
Psychomotor Area	Sensory stimulation	• Learn to plan
	Space-time perception	• Practice self-control and tolerate frustration
	Corporal awareness	• Learn to find solutions to problems
Cognitive Area	Atention and concentration	• Assume responsibility
	Recognition of categories	• Learn to express interest in others
	Memory	• Develop the ability to connect to others' feelings and understand them
	Language and communication	• Improve verbal and non-verbal communication
Social-emotional Area	Presentation	• Express emotions and feelings
	Activity	• Develop self-motivation
	Leave-taking and relaxation	• Develop capacity to generate and enjoy positive feelings
	Board games	• Develop socially enhancing behavior

SOCIALIZATION

CHAIN THE GREETINGS

The objective of this activity is for the RIs to introduce themselves to the group, and to greet the dog.

The AIT introduces himself, saying his own name and that of the dog in a strong voice. Then he invites the RIs to introduce themselves to the animal.

The IP begins the activity by setting the example: he introduces himself to the dog and greets him by performing a particular action.

Then he chooses one of the seated RIs, extending his hand to help him up. The RI approaches the dog, says his own name out loud and imitates the action just performed by the IP before carrying out a different action of his own.

Then he chooses one of the other participants, who rises and goes through the same drill.

This activity, a sort of "chain" of greetings, can have as many "links" as we want, and can be made more or less demanding according to the circumstances.

The dog's participation is limited to performing the requested skills or tricks, or merely observing the participants' actions.

The AIT oversees and instructs the dog from a distance.

COMMANDS FOR THE DOG	MATERIALS
• Stand • Stay • Various tricks and skills	• Skills cards

	Physical coordination	Objectives
Psychomotor Area	Sensory stimulation	• Exercise sight-body coordination
	Space-time perception	• Exercise tactile perception
	Corporal awareness	• Develop mental image of body structure
Cognitive Area	Atention and concentration	• Exercise observation of objects in space
	Recognition of categories	• Pay attention to movements of others
	Memory	• Acquire or exercise the ability to imitate
	Language and communication	• Stimulate group communication and interaction
Social-emotional Area	Presentation	• Learn and respect social norms
	Activity	• Explore different means of communication
	Leave-taking and relaxation	• Express fantasies
	Board games	

SOCIALIZATION

COMMUNICATING WITH STATIC

The objective of this activity is for two RIs to be able to effectively communicate despite acoustic interference from the rest of the group.

We choose two RIs: one will be the sender and the other the receiver of a certain message, for example, the part of the dog's body the receiver must touch.

The other participants in the session take their place between the two RIs and, by way of shouts, arm-waving or other movements try to prevent the sender and receiver from communicating.

The two protagonists must try to establish visual contact and raise their voices above the interference in order to get the message across the divide.

After a couple minutes, the AIT walks the dog over to the receiver so he can touch the body part transmitted in the message.

If it is the correct part, both the sender and the receiver get to give the dog a treat.

The game continues with another pair.

COMMANDS FOR THE DOG	MATERIALS
• Stay	• Cards with instructions
• Heel	
• Treat	
• Various tricks and skills	

		Objectives
Psychomotor Area	Physical coordination	• Association: stimulate group cooperation
	Sensory stimulation	• Learn and respect social norms
	Space-time perception	• Explore different means of communication
	Corporal awareness	• Stimulate group communication and interaction
Cognitive Area	Atention and concentration	• Experience the pleasure of laughter
	Recognition of categories	• Experience the shedding of inhibitions
	Memory	
	Language and communication	
Social-emotional Area	Presentation	
	Activity	
	Leave-taking and relaxation	
	Board games	

The objective of this activity is for the RI to take part in a new form of communication and, in so doing, discover the action that either the IP or the other RIs have decided he should perform.

The refrain is "cold-warm-hot" and is delivered with the clicker. When the RI hears a click, it means he's going in the right direction. If he hears no click, it means he's going in the wrong direction or off-track. The RI, by trial and error, finds out what action is required of him. We must impress upon the RIs the importance of emitting, and perceiving, the clicks at the right moment so as to not give or receive false indicators.

The required actions can be of varying difficulty: touch a certain part of the body of a particular dog, change the dog's collar, hug or pat on the back a companion, give the leash to a certain participant, etc.

When the RI discovers his task and performs it, his companions congratulate him and the dog does a trick for him.

Variations:

– Use this game to explain a dog's way of perceiving. When we stand in front of the dog with a clicker, it means we want him to learn a trick or skill. We emphasize the importance of our body language, of our self-assuredness when giving a command and the ability to reward by way of the clicker at the right time.

COMMANDS FOR THE DOG	MATERIALS
• Various tricks	• Clicker

	Physical coordination	Objectives
Psychomotor Area	Sensory stimulation	• Develop self-motivation
	Space-time perception	• Improve decision-making capability
	Corporal awareness	• Explore different forms of communication: mime, rhythmic, figurative, dramatic
Cognitive Area	Atention and concentration	• Foment positive group dynamic
	Recognition of categories	• Exercise listening skills and powers of observation
	Memory	• Experience the shedding of inhibitions
	Language and communication	• Exercise sight-body coordination
Social-emotional Area	Presentation	
	Activity	
	Leave-taking and relaxation	
	Board games	

GROUP INTRODUCTIONS

The objective of this activity is for the RIs to interact among themselves and introduce their dogs.

The RIs take their places in a semi-circle around the AIT, who introduces himself and each one of his dogs. After saying each dog's name, mentions a particular trait of that animal.

Then the AIT has the dog go to an RI, who must introduce himself to the rest of the group by saying his name and one of his own particular characteristics in a loud and clear voice. Once the round of introductions is completed, the AIT assigns a dog to each participant at random. If the dog is small, he can put it on the RI's lap or on a stool in order to promote maximum physical contact.

Then the AIT asks the group who the person is who has a certain dog in his arms. He invites him to tell the group what it feels like to hold the dog on his lap, what he would like to do with the animal, etc. The AIT then asks the entire group who would like to pick up and hold that dog. The person who responds raises his hand and politely asks his companion if he will let him hold the dog.

We continue the activity until all the RIs have held all the dogs.

Variations:

   – Every time a dog is passed, the RI receiving him puts an item of clothing on him.

COMMANDS FOR THE DOG	MATERIALS
• Stay	• Treats
• Treat	
• Look	

366

	Physical coordination	Objectives
Psychomotor Area	Sensory stimulation	• Expression of emotions and feelings
	Space-time perception	• Verbal and non-verbal communication
	Corporal awareness	• Develop capacity to generate positive feelings
Cognitive Area	Atention and concentration	• Develop capacity to enjoy positive feelings
	Recognition of categories	• Develop self-motivation
	Memory	• Augment personal and social well-being
	Language and communication	• Experience the pleasure of laughter
Social-emotional Area	Presentation	• Stimulate socialization
	Activity	• Exercise tactile perception
	Leave-taking and relaxation	• Develop or evaluate long-term memory
	Board games	

SOCIALIZATION

WE ALL DRESS HIM UP

The objective of this activity is to dress up the dog while identifying and describing the items of clothing.

With the dog in the 'down' position and the RIs around him, we begin by brushing and petting him.

Then the IP hands out an item of clothing to each RI. Taking turns, the all name the item they got.

The IP asks who wants to put a certain piece of clothing on the dog.

Whoever has that item describes it for the rest of the group, then puts it on the dog.

The IP proceeds in that fashion, asking about another piece of clothing, until all present have put their item on the dog.

Variations:

– In pairs, the RIs select two of the same item of clothing, but of different sizes. The goal is for them to discuss which of the two is more appropriate and why it is better than the other for a certain dog taking part in the session, or for a dog of a certain breed like the one in a photograph.

– The RI takes from each of the pockets on the CTAC dog blanket a card with a description or a riddle referring to an item of clothing. After naming the item, he and the dog go around the room looking for that item. When they find it, the RI puts it on the dog.

COMMANDS FOR THE DOG	MATERIALS
• Sit	• Clothes for dressing the dog
• Down	• Brushes
• Stay	

368

	Physical coordination	Objectives
Psychomotor Area	Sensory stimulation	• Introductions
	Space-time perception	• Develop capacity to enjoy positive feelings
	Corporal awareness	• Create affective bonds
Cognitive Area	Atention and concentration	• Exercise fine motor skills
	Recognition of categories	• Enrich vocabulary
	Memory	• Learn and respect social norms
	Language and communication	• Stimulate physical contact and interaction
Social-emotional Area	Presentation	• Cooperation: Stimulate helpful relationships
	Activity	• Accept norms of social interaction
	Leave-taking and relaxation	
	Board games	

THE STAGES OF LIFE

The objective of this activity is for the RI to identify the stages of a dog's life so as to be able to draw a parallel with the stages of human life.

To begin, we place three dogs of differing ages on three tables of differing height: the youngest dog on the lowest table, and the oldest on the highest.

The AIT introduces each dog and narrates a version of his life story with the aid of photographs showing the various stages of a dog's life and his activities in each stage.

Then we distribute the photos among the RIs who, taking turns, approach the dog whose age is closest to the one in the picture, talk to him and pet him before setting the photograph down on that table.

A fourth, empty table can be present as a way to talk about the death of an elderly dog that the RIs knew, of the grief we felt at his passing and the fact that, although he is no longer physically present, we continue to hold him in our memory.

Variations:

– Draw parallels between the life and activities of dogs at different points in their lives and our own lives and activities.

– Talk about people or pets who have died but who we cherish in our memories for the important role they played in our lives.

COMMANDS FOR THE DOG	MATERIALS
• Down • Stay	• Four tables of different heights • Photos of chronological stages of dog's life • Photos of chronological stages of human life • Series of photographs of canine activities • Series of photographs of human activities

		Objectives
Psychomotor Area	Physical coordination	• Stimulate group communication and interaction
	Sensory stimulation	• Discover elements of the social life of adults
	Space-time perception	• Stimulate active listening
	Corporal awareness	• Learn to listen and respond
Cognitive Area	Atention and concentration	• Improve verbal expression
	Recognition of categories	• Express feelings
	Memory	
	Language and communication	
Social-emotional Area	Presentation	
	Activity	
	Leave-taking and relaxation	
	Board games	

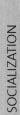

SOCIALIZATION

NO-ASKING PUZZLES

The objective of this activity is for the RI to complete a puzzle with the help of his companions but without asking them for the puzzle pieces.

We have as many different dog-breed puzzles as RIs taking part in the game.

The AIT gives each RI a piece from one puzzle so the player knows which is "his." Then the technician distributes the remaining pieces of all the puzzles at random among the players.

Now the RIs concentrate on putting their particular puzzles together, but with the condition that they may not ask, either by word or gesture, their mates for the pieces they need. Each one must simply wait until the others give him the pieces pertaining to his puzzle.

Once the puzzles are completed, we can talk about the dogs they portray: the breed, its strong and weak points, the kind of job it is most suited for or anecdotes the RIs may have regarding similar dogs, anything that stimulates communication among the group members.

Then the group lists the same number of dog tricks as pieces in the puzzle. They take turns having the dog (or dogs) perform the tricks without repeating any of them while one of the participants activates the clicker when the dog has successfully performed the action.

Variations:

– The dog delivers the puzzle pieces in his mouth. The RI, when receiving a piece, must engage with a companion, or the IP, to either ask or answer a question regarding emotions, such as: "What do you like?" or "What makes you sad?"

COMMANDS FOR THE DOG	MATERIALS
• Various tricks and skills	• Various dog-breed puzzles with the same number of pieces • Clicker

	Physical coordination	Objectives
Psychomotor Area	Sensory stimulation	• Pay attention to movements of others
	Space-time perception	• Acquire or exercise the ability to concentrate
	Corporal awareness	• Recognize parts of a whole
Cognitive Area	Atention and concentration	• Learn and respect social norms
	Recognition of categories	• Stimulate socialization
	Memory	• Cooperation: Stimulate helpful relationships
	Language and communication	• Association: Stimulate group cooperation
Social-emotional Area	Presentation	• Explore different means of communication
	Activity	• Improve verbal expression
	Leave-taking and relaxation	
	Board games	

BODY LANGUAGE

The objective of this exercise is to describe and interpret the dog's body language for insight into his mood and foster the RI's empathy with the animal.

This will also help us explore our own body language as manifested in our changing moods or state of mind, thus increasing our self-awareness.

And finally, this activity encourages the RI to be conscious of the importance of his body language when interacting and communicating with the dog. We can then extend this concept to inter-personal relationships as a way of fomenting mutual respect and empathy.

Before beginning, we establish three rules for correctly interpreting a dog's body language.

1. We must "read" all the animal's simultaneous postures and gestures as a whole. Even so, at the outset we will concentrate on understanding what is being expressed by the main parts of the dog's body.

2. Interpret the postures and gestures in context. All the animal's gestures must be understood in the context in which they are made. But we must keep in mind that, in order to correctly interpret people's body language, we must be aware of the following point.

3. Observation of coherence. The success of the interpretation stems from observing the coherence, or lack thereof, between the set of postures and gestures and the verbal expression along with the overall body language.

COMMANDS FOR THE DOG	MATERIALS
• Stay • Get it • Down • Hide • Speak • Bang • Back • No! • Mark 	• CTAC cards of canine body language • Cards or charts of human body language • Emotions cards • Cards or brief situational narratives for role-playing activities

		Objectives
Psychomotor Area	Physical coordination	• Exercise visual perception: background-figure • Develop mental image of body structure • Perceive facial gestures • Pay attention to movements of others • Acquire or exercise symbolic thinking • Acquire or exercise ability to concentrate • Establish relationships • Develop the symbolic function • Develop capacity for observation • Stimulate the imagination, socialization
	Sensory stimulation	
	Space-time perception	
	Corporal awareness	
Cognitive Area	Atention and concentration	
	Recognition of categories	
	Memory	
	Language and communication	
Social-emotional Area	Presentation	
	Activity	
	Leave-taking and relaxation	
	Board games	

SOCIALIZATION

WHO'S THE ONE?

. . . .

The objective of this activity is for the RI to be surprised and impressed by the dog's capabilities as a way of strengthening the bond between them.

We hand over to the group of RIs an object relating to the dog: a kerchief, a leash, a hoop or a ball, and we have the participants circulate around the room while passing the object around from one to another. At a certain point, the IP tells them to sit down in a semi-circle.

The RI holding the object at that point puts it down on the floor before the arrayed players.

The IP, who has worked this out beforehand with the AIT, sits either to the right of the RI who put down the object, or at any point in the semi-circle but adopting the same posture as that RI.

Then we invite the AIT and the dog to enter the room.

The AIT tells the participants that this dog has a super-power: that either he can see through walls, or he can read people's minds.

If we use the seeing-through-walls power, as soon as the dog enters he goes right over to the person who placed the object on the floor.

If we use the telepathy option, we ask all the RIs to repeat silently in their minds the name of the individual who put down the object. The dog sits before the RIs and next to the technician and "whispers" into the AIT'sear the physical characteristics of the person who last held the object. Those without these traits are thus eliminated from consideration, until the person who deposited the object is revealed.

If we want to emphasize the acuity of the dog's sense of smell, we have him sniff each of the RIs upon entering the room. He then sits down in front of the one who last touched the object.

COMMANDS FOR THE DOG	MATERIALS
• Sit	• Dog grooming items
• Stay	• An accomplice
• Search	
• Look	
• Speak	
• Head down	

	Physical coordination	Objectives
Psychomotor Area	Sensory stimulation	• Acquire or exercise ability to concentrate
	Space-time perception	• Learn companions' names
	Corporal awareness	• Stimulate socialization
Cognitive Area	Atention and concentration	• Learn and respect social norms • Foster sense of group responsibility
	Recognition of categories	• Stimulate group communication and interaction
	Memory	• Play with concepts of intuition and mystery
	Language and communication	• Develop capacity to enjoy positive feelings
Social-emotional Area	Presentation	
	Activity	
	Leave-taking and relaxation	
	Board games	

PICK A CARD

The objective of this activity is for the RI to be positively surprised by the dog's ability as a way of fostering the bond between them.

The AIT has a deck of CTAC theme cards that he will use to do magic tricks. With the dog's help, he will guess which card the RI has picked.

Sight trick

The AIT invites the RI to pick a card from the deck and, after looking at it, replace it in the stack. Just then, the AIT discreetly peeks at the card beneath which the RI has slipped his card. The AIT then takes from the deck several cards at random, making sure that the one the RI picked is among them, and lays them face down on the table.

Then he asks the RI to rest his head against that of the dog and concentrate on the card he picked so the dog can "read" his mind and guess the right card. The dog, taking tips from the technician, then proceeds to mark and eliminate one card after another until the one remaining is the one the RI had picked.

Rotation trick

The RI picks a card from the deck, looks at it, then passes it over the dog's head in a circle before replacing it in the stack. The AIT starts showing the cards one by one and when the card picked by the RI comes up, the dog barks. For the trick to work, the AIT must have:

– Had all the cards facing the same way when the deck was presented.

– Observed whether the RI, after withdrawing the card, turned it 180° or replaced it without turning it around. If he didn't turn it, the AIT must discreetly do so. If he did turn it, the one he picked will be the only one upside-down.

COMMANDS FOR THE DOG	MATERIALS
• Sit • Stay • Head down • Mark it • Look 	• Deck of CTAC theme cards of skills and activities

		Objectives
Psychomotor Area	Physical coordination	
	Sensory stimulation	• Pay attention to the movements of others
	Space-time perception	• Acquire or exercise ability to concentrate
	Corporal awareness	• Improve oral comprehension
Cognitive Area	Atention and concentration	• Develop or evaluate short-term memory
	Recognition of categories	• Learn and respect social norms
	Memory	• Exercise sight-body coordination
	Language and communication	• Play with intuition and mystery
Social-emotional Area	Presentation	• Associate, cooperate
		• Experience the pleasure of guessing correctly
	Activity	• Experience the pleasure of being surprised
	Leave-taking and relaxation	
	Board games	

SOCIALIZATION

CROSS AT THE LIGHT

The objective of this activity is for the RI to identify and respond correctly to the colors of a traffic light in order to be able to cross the street safely.

The group lines up on a corner with a traffic light in the following order: the AIT, the dog, the RI and the IP. They wait for the green that will allow them to cross.

Before stepping into the street, we ask the RI to focus his attention on the light and say whether it is green or red.

When he has said the current color of the light, we introduce these two brief key phrases, repeating them several times and adding a gesture for each before asking the RI to pronounce them to the dog: "Green, go," and "Red, stay."

When the RI sees that the light is red and emits the order "Red, stay" by either gesture or voice, the IP gives him a treat to give to the dog who sits waiting by his side. When the light turns and the RI says, "Green, go," they all cross the street. Upon reaching the opposite sidewalk, the IP gives the RI a treat to give to the dog.

Aids:

– Previous work in the classroom with the colors red and green.
– Previous work in the classroom with starting to walk and halting, according to colors.
– Use of a red or green flashlight or beam that the IP moves from near the RI toward the traffic light as a means of directing the RI's sight to the light.
– Red and green pockets on either side of the walking vest in which we will place red or green chips or treats as a way to give the RI a physical representation of the traffic light's colors.

COMMANDS FOR THE DOG	MATERIALS
• Heel	• Autism walking vest with red and green pockets
• Treat	• Red and green signals
• Stay	• Treats
	• Curbs

	Physical coordination	Objectives
Psychomotor Area	Sensory stimulation	• Exercise fine and gross motor skills
	Space-time perception	• Exercise sight-space perception
	Corporal awareness	• Exercise visual perception: background-figure
Cognitive Area	Atention and concentration	• Foment responsibility
	Recognition of categories	• Pay attention to instructions
	Memory	• Acquire or exercise notion of colors
	Language and communication	• Stimulate socialization
Social-emotional Area	Presentation	• Learn and respect social norms
	Activity	• Discover elements of the social life of adults
	Leave-taking and relaxation	• Experience the pleasure of achievement
	Board games	• Acquire or exercise symbolic thinking
		• Acquire or exercise ability to concentrate

The objective of this workshop is for the RI to learn good personal grooming and hygiene habits, encouraged by the presence of and interaction with the dog.

This will require multiple sessions in order for the RI and the dog to get to know each other and to form an affective bond.

Introduction and photographic mural: After the workshop team introduces itself by answering three questions (who am I, what do I like, what do I not like), we make a photographic and chronological mural illustrating the RI's relationship with the dog. Below each photo, the RI writes a brief impression regarding the activity portrayed, about himself, etc.

Approaching the dog and handling of tools: We follow the standard routines for bringing the dog and the RI together so he can pet the animal and enjoy his proximity. We show him the accessories used in handling the dog, to foster the RI's sense of autonomy regarding the dog during the sessions.

Basic knowledge of canine anatomy and psychology:

Using some of the exercises presented in this manual, we show the RI,

- The parts of the dog's body
- How to brush him: for example, the technique of three strokes with the grain to untangle, three against the grain to remove shed hair, three more with the grain to smooth.
- Notions of the dog's body language: fear, anger, happiness, relaxation...

COMMANDS FOR THE DOG	MATERIALS
• Head down	• Collar, leash, working harness
• Sit	• Various brushes
• Down	• Camera
• Look	• Mural paper
• Stay	• CTAC emotions cards
• Heel	• CTAC canine anatomy cards
• Treat	• Interactive die
• Shame	
• Curtsy	
• Kiss	

	Physical coordination	Objectives
Psychomotor Area	Sensory stimulation	• Develop capacity for self-motivation
	Space-time perception	• Exercise gross and fine motor skills
	Corporal awareness	• Exercise sense of left-right and sense of overall body movement
Cognitive Area	Atention and concentration	• Observation of natural phenomena
	Recognition of categories	• Listening and responding
	Memory	• Improve language comprehension and expression
	Language and communication	• Stimulate group interaction and communication
Social-emotional Area	Presentation	• Create an effective bond and foster affinities
	Activity	• Expression and management of emotions and feelings
	Leave-taking and relaxation	
	Board games	

SOCIALIZATION

The objective of this section is for the RI to assume responsibility, to the greatest degree possible, for the care and grooming of the therapy dog.

According to the this premise: "Your friend, the dog, needs your help in taking care of himself, and there are several things he must do before he can come here to visit you and play with you."

Presentation and use of the canine grooming kit

The AIT identifies, exhibits and briefly explains the use of the items that make up a canine grooming kit. Before moving on, the RIs learn that the objects must be used in a respectful manner and that they must be used the right way. He also learns the physical and social benefits they provide the dog.

A photographic mural of the accessories for canine grooming, and their relationship to implements that serve similar functions in human grooming. We make the associations first with illustrations or photos of the dog's tools, then with an image of the corresponding item used in personal hygiene by humans.

– Materials and activities
– Various types of hair brushes
– Toothbrush, canine toothpaste
– Moist towelettes for washing the external parts of the ear
– Nail clipper (without blade) for demonstrating how we cut the dog's nails
– Nail file, for showing how to file the nails
– Shampoo, dry shampoo, cologne, moisturizing cream, hair dryer, etc.

When the dog is clean and groomed, in light of the goal set for the day, the RI may have him perform a trick or skill, then spend some relaxing time with him.

COMMANDS FOR THE DOG	MATERIALS
• Fetch	• Brushes
• Drop	• Toothbrush or brush worn on finger
• Give	
• Come	• Canine toothpaste
• Stay	• Towel
• Belly	• Moist towelettes
• Down	• Items of human personal hygiene
• Stand	

		Objectives
Psychomotor Area	Physical coordination	
	Sensory stimulation	• Exercise gross and fine motor skills
	Space-time perception	• Learn and respect social norms
	Corporal awareness	• Cooperation: encourage helpful relationships
Cognitive Area	Atention and concentration	• Enhance tactile recognition
	Recognition of categories	• Enhance verbal expression
	Memory	• Encourage affinities
	Language and communication	• Create an affective bond
Social-emotional Area	Presentation	• Develop positive social conduct
	Activity	• Work responsibly
	Leave-taking and relaxation	• Learn to plan
	Board games	

SOCIALIZATION

The objective of this section is for the RI to learn to take care of his personal hygiene and grooming on his own, based on the following premise: "All the things we have learned and done in taking care of the dog, things that have served to make the dog happy, can be applied to ourselves, to put ourselves in good condition before going out for a walk with the dog."

The RI's grooming kit and clothes

The IP presents a toiletries pouch to the RI as a gift. Over the course of the sessions, the RI will use the pouch to store the various items used in human personal hygiene and grooming.

To begin, the AIT performs a certain action on the dog (i.e. brushing), which the RI describes, also commenting on the benefits it provides the animal.

The RI then performs the equivalent action on himself, using an item provided by the IP.

While he does this, they talk about how this activity is correctly performed, when and how many times a day it is done and the specific benefits it provides the individual.

As the RI becomes more adept at his own grooming, he will have enough time to first groom the dog before taking care of himself.

Things to work on:

– Washing hands with soap and water after the session
– Combing or fixing one's hair, with or without accessories
– Cleaning of the teeth with brush, toothpaste and dental floss
– Use of deodorant
– Manicure and pedicure (moisturizing, trimming and filing of nails)
– Make-up, shaving, hair removal
– Clothing

Reward:
If the RI does a good job, he may then go for a walk with the dog.

COMMANDS FOR THE DOG	MATERIALS
• Fetch	• Canine grooming tools
• Drop and give	• Human grooming tools
• Stay	• Toiletries pouch
• Down	• Leash
• Heel	

	Physical coordination	Objectives
Psychomotor Area	Sensory stimulation	• Exercise fine motor skills
	Space-time perception	• Exercise tactile and olfactory perception
	Corporal awareness	• Acquire or exercise the ability to imitate
Cognitive Area	Atention and concentration	• Learn and respect social norms
	Recognition of categories	• Discover the social life of the adult world
	Memory	• Accept norms of social interaction
	Language and communication	• Develop an accurate and positive self-image
Social-emotional Area	Presentation	• Acknowledge one's own needs
	Activity	• Develop capacity for self-motivation
	Leave-taking and relaxation	
	Board games	

DOG "CHUTES AND LADDERS"

The objective is to advance along the oversized playing board, carrying out the various actions described in the boxes, until reaching the finish line.

Before starting the game, the AIT completes a circuit (degree of complexity may vary) with the dog while the RIs pay close attention in case they are called upon to repeat it.

We draw on the floor or on a mat a series of boxes bounded by a starting line and a finish line. The dog fulfills the function of the die, effecting a certain number of barks or doing a trick a certain number of times to indicate how many places the player should advance. The playing pieces are figurines of different breeds of dog. Each RI chooses his piece, identifies it and describes it.

Then the game begins, with the players taking turns and following the rules as they advance.

The boxes are marked with instructions such as the following:

1- Tell a story about an experience with a pet.
2- From dog to dog: the RI advances to box 9.
3- Have the dog do a trick. If he does it correctly, advance two boxes.
4- Tell something you like about yourself.
5- Tell something that others do to you that bothers you.
6- Repeat the circuit the AIT made before the game began.
7- Maze of leashes: Lose a turn.
8- Throw the dog a ball.
9- From dog to dog: Return to box 2.
10-Three steps in the right direction with the clicker: Each time the dog touches the RI's hand, he makes a click or asks a companion to do so.
11- Brush the dog with a friend: The RI must politely ask a companion to help him brush the dog, while the others pay close attention.
12- Give a treat to each companion, to be used in having the dog perform a trick or skill.
13- Empty bowl: Start over from the beginning.
14- Pay a compliment to each companion, then one to the dog in exchange for a treat or a trick.
15- Hug the dog.
16- Repeat the box you like the best.

COMMANDS FOR THE DOG	MATERIALS
• Get it	• Mat
• Speak	• Markers (felt-tipped pens)
• Various tricks and skills	• Brushes
• Fetch	• Balls
• Give	• Treats

	Physical coordination	Objectives
Psychomotor Area	Sensory stimulation	• Exercise gross and fine motor skills
	Space-time perception	• Acquire or exercise sense of space and direction
	Corporal awareness	• Acquire or exercise ability to concentrate
Cognitive Area	Atention and concentration	• Pay attention to instructions and to movements
	Recognition of categories	• Visually recognize numbers
	Memory	• Learn and respect social norms
	Language and communication	• Experience the pleasure of achievement
Social-emotional Area	Presentation	• Experience the pleasure of laughter
	Activity	• Learn to take turns
	Leave-taking and relaxation	• Augment social and personal wellbeing
	Board games	

15905665R00221

Made in the USA
San Bernardino, CA
11 October 2014